SAINTS IN DUE SEASON

Essays On The Art Of Christian Aging

Thomas P. McDonnell

Library of Congress Catalog Card No. 83-60742
ISBN 0-87973-623-2
PRINTED IN THE UNITED STATES OF AMERICA

OUR SUNDAY VISITOR, INC.
HUNTINGTON

Contents

Dedication

To the women in my life:

Elizabeth: wife and truest friend;
Mary Kathleen: daughter of our joy;
Sophia Veronica: mother, student and teacher;
Leora: Sister Montfort de La Croix, so early blessed;
Sophie Therese: sister and companion in faith;
Kateri Tekakwitha: comfort in our affliction;
Edith Stein: who bore the cross of our time;
Mary: source of all inspiration.

Epigraphs

The Lord lifts up all who are falling
and raises up all who are bowed down.
The eyes of all look hopefully to you,
and you give them their food in due season.
—The New American Bible

How many things by season season'd are
To their right praise and true perfection!
—Shakespeare, **The Merchant of Venice**

It is one of the chief things that I owe to my fortune, that my
bodily state has run its course, each part in its due season. I
have seen it in the herb, in the flower, and in the fruit; and
now I see it in decay. Happily, however, since it was
according to Nature. I bear my present infirmities much
the more patiently because they are in season, and because
they invoke a more kindly recollection of the long happiness
of my past life.
—Montaigne, **Essays**
Translated by E.J. Trechmann, Oxford University Press

Foreword

HOW paradoxical it is that as our friends grow older we can give them less. Young people are the best receivers by far: their enthusiasm is great, their interests are numerous and may change rapidly, and their capacity to appreciate kindness is at its peak. Similarly, the middle-aged are good receivers, too: their interests may have grown fewer, but their focus is usually and comfortably narrowed, while those who would gift them know just which tiny gap in an enthusiasm needs yet to be filled. It is relatively easy to give to those enjoying the morning and the noontime of life.

But what of those friends of the afternoon and evening, those who have passed through life's mid-day and now turn toward the twilight? For most, the vibrancy of interest that characterizes youth has diminished, while for man, wants and needs—as the popular song has it—have indeed dwindled down to a precious few. Hence the paradox: those whom we would gladly shower with gifts and kindnesses and tokens of our love—they are the ones who require less, who are content with little. We often have trouble finding a gift that will both please and uplift them at once.

In this book, Thomas P. McDonnell has helped all of us in our quest to please and edify those of our friends who are "getting along" in life. He has compiled a series of attractive essays on Christian aging which, based on the lives of ten saints whom he especially reveres, relates the sheer practicality of goodness to the ongoing quest for personal sanctity. Though his saints are familiar and well-known persons—Mary, Francis, Thomas More, and others—the author has retold their familiar stories in such a way as to offer particular relevance and solace to our friends of the twilight years. If Mary, Thomas and the rest were familiar figures before, they will be even more familiar, and beloved, when the pages that follow are finished.

As an experienced writer and critic (now himself officially retired from Catholic journalism), the author weaves into the fabric of his essays pertinent quotes and anecdotes from other writers, other critics, and often from the saintly subjects of his work, as well. The essays have sparkle, tenderness, and a deep respect for the experiences, the viewpoints, the pains, and the visions of those now along in years. Given his potential readership, he has here shelved the paraphernalia of scholarship, blending hints of further reading and the citation of sources into the text proper. It is a considerate thing to do.

To the wealth of material already published on the saints from every conceivable aspect—saints for children, for the ill, for the parents-to-be, for the downcast, for the modern woman, and the like—Mr. McDonnell has now added a collection designed especially for the older, the aging, the infinitely wiser Christian reader. That, too, was a considerate thing to do, and I both compliment the author for writing *Saints In Due Season* and recommend his thoughtful essays to a general public I know will be appreciative.

✠Humberto Cardinal Medeiros
Archbishop of Boston

Saints In Their Maturity

An Introduction

PEOPLE in their maturity is a preferable phrase, let us say, even at the risk of indulging a euphemism, because a lump sum like "The Elderly" seems such a final and dispensable category. It is easy to forget about people who are locked away in convenient categories. When you are elderly or maturing, however, you are still engaged in the human process of growth and development — and *that,* despite all the propaganda to the contrary, is something exciting to contemplate. Contemplation itself, in fact (though not, it is hoped, as a scare term), will prove to be part and parcel of what this book is about. If we realize at least this much to begin with, then perhaps we can go on to use the terms "elderly" and "the elderly" in their conventional usage, while at the same time remaining open to the suggested alternatives.

The epigraphs for our title's theme are not mere decorations. They have been searched for with great care and found with even greater delight. Today we live to average life-spans that by far exceed those of Michel de Montaigne's and Shakespeare's days; but whereas they and many others before our own time have written about old age with candor and an eternally refreshing sense of our human reality, we, on the

1

other hand, in the enlightenment of the twentieth century and its predominantly youth-centered culture, avoid at all costs those reprehensible and fearful terms "old age" and its consequence "death." These are the great unmentionables of our age. We live on the illusions of a consumer society that is forever seeking its own rejuvenation.

Saints, however, are the supreme realists. This is why we have linked — more than linked, have enjoined — the lives and careers of the saints with the supreme adventure of growing old. We shall all become saints in due season, granting the necessary grace to do so, but the saints themselves are those practical guides without whom we should perhaps fail to ascend the holy mountain. We too often forget this aspect of the saints — that they are the ultimate pragmatists and not all mystical fluff and mere inspiration. They inspire only when we think we can climb no higher. The extreme pieties of the past have given the saints a bad name.

So it is all the more pleasant to notice that hagiography, or writings on the lives of the saints, has become a renewed Catholic growth industry. After a trendy lull of benign disdain, following what was presumed to have been the heady new liberties released by Vatican Council II, saints are back again. Saints, indeed, have always been one of the chief glories of the Church. We are the best in the world at producing people of certified sanctity — from all those curious and sometimes little-known Blesseds to the grand illuminations of the many saints themselves, and of course we use them for every occasion.

There are patron saints for every affliction or situation, from aching teeth to lost objects, and all the occupations have their saints—gardeners, cooks and even traveling salesmen. The categories have become so extensive that the book publishers are now issuing collections for all kinds of tastes and attitudes, and so it is all the more surprising that we have not yet had a "Saints for the Elderly"—or would it be more euphemistic and salable to say something like "Saints for the Slightly Growing Old" and even "Saints for the More or Less Mature"? But may God chastise anyone who dares to suggest a "Saints for Senior Citizens." This last demeaning category, were it ever to come to pass, would have to be a fully computerized production compiled and edited by a committee of certified bureaucrats clinically immune to the great humanity of the saints.

Seriously, is it possible at all to deal with the question of saints for the elderly? There are some difficulties at hand, I think, that ought to be more than casually considered. Again, of course, there is the difficulty that we happen to live in a country not too well disposed toward the problems of old people, as we must sooner or later call them, which is to say, from age sixty or sixty-five onward. How do you think those over sixty-five must feel when they are faced, for instance, by a political threat that Social Security could be cut as a means to lower a federal budget? It can send chills through people who can barely manage to get by on low fixed incomes and minimal pensions. The anxieties of the old are often taken to be a manifestation of a merely cantankerous nature, whereas in fact we more often than not have something to be thoroughly cantankerous about. We are not expendable. Listen to Evelyn Eaton Whitehead and James D. Whitehead in *Christian Life Patterns* (Doubleday Image Books, 1982), which ought to be required reading on the subject:

3

It is not easy to be old in America. Growing older seems an affront to one's self-image, a deterrent to one's plans, and a general inconvenience to society. The fact that aging is inevitable does little to soften its negative aspect. . . . And yet there are hints that this negative story of aging is not the full account. Most of us hope for a long life, even though we are ambiguous about being old.

There is yet another difficulty, however, having to do with any proposal of saints for the elderly, which must bring us very close to the heart of the matter. I mean by this that it has less to do with conditions beyond one's control, such as the vast complexities of the economic order, and more to do with the question of what it means to be old — or "eldering" — and approaching that point of spiritual metamorphosis we call death. Saints for the young are easy to summon, God knows, for at that stage of life there are more than enough role-models to go around. There's nothing but the future in the offing; and inspirations everywhere, like wild flowers by the side of the road, are there for the picking. By adulthood, we have already settled on this or that favorite saint and are on our way. But when you are old, if you think that retirement age is particularly old, it is nevertheless high time you thought of becoming your own saint! Your own salvation is at stake and therefore your own sainthood would seem quite enough to deal with. When you are advancing in years, moreover, and getting perhaps a little crusty around the edges, it isn't likely that you'll have started begging intercessions from all those other childlike saints in the wings. Kids, however beautiful, but still kids. You will need saints, if at all, who have been around and who know the score.

Besides, there's still another problem and a somewhat touchy one at that. The Whiteheads recognize this problem almost at once in having posed the question, "Holiness: hazardous to your health?" and claim in response, "There is a strong tradition in the Christian and Jewish experience that holiness is dangerous and potentially destructive." Maybe this is why it has always been puzzling to ordinary people when a very holy sister or an exemplary priest would say to us, without any hint of affectation, "Pray for me." But if, then, as the experts suggest, the spiritual life puts a strain on our health, does this mean that holiness is out of the question for the elderly? I think almost the opposite is true — that holiness in maturity is not to be gainsaid on any terms of, as the Whiteheads themselves conclude, "Holiness, like health, is ultimately success at living."

What we have been doing in these few introductory paragraphs is simply clearing the air and setting some necessary values in order. The point is that the elderly ought to meet the saints pretty much on their (the elderly's) own terms, for it is they who are most immediately concerned with the shaping of their own salvation. If the greatest tragedy is not to have become a saint, as that superb French novelist Leon Bloy once said, then the elderly would be well advised to receive these saints—meaning especially the ones in this book—like honored guests or welcome visitors in the late afternoon. It is not holiness at a late stage that is dangerous to your health, but learning in a new and painfully revealing way something you were sure you already knew.

There is no strict conformity in these essays to what the heart and mind may seek out as part of the great adventure of advancing into the interior and, if possible, ascending the holy mountain for the overview and perhaps a backward glance to where we had been

5

so brief a time ago. There's nothing like a mountaintop to give you some idea of where, as the young moderns say, you are coming from. Above all, this is not hagiography in either the limited or the pietistic sense. A brief biographical sketch is provided at the beginning of each essay on a given saint in order to establish in at least some minimal way the most salient facts of time and place concerning the subject at hand. If you are looking for strictly biographical materials, however, you are herewith duly advised to seek elsewhere in any number of fine dictionaries of the saints or, better still, in selected biographies — a few of which are recommended in the suggested reading lists at the end of each chapter.

The point I want to make clear is that these saints—Monica, John Vianney, Teresa of Avila, Jerome, Francis of Assisi, Job, Joseph, Thomas More, John the Apostle and Mary—are also our companions and fellow pilgrims for a journey whose end is nearly in sight. Saints are held largely in awe at points of life which are something other than fully developed or which have not been touched with a sense of the divine folly of things. I have an intuition that the saints are better company than we generally take them to be—that is, as characters full of piety and flaunting killjoy attitudes—and I say this on the possibility that I may have met and known one. I mean the late Thomas Merton, the Cistercian monk and contemplative of Gethsemani Abbey in Kentucky, who was one of the easiest of persons to be with and one who, after the first five minutes in his company, you would swear you had known all your life. I have a notion that people who turn out to be saints are very much like that. You would think that their soul-to-soul insights would put you ill at ease, but it is exactly the opposite effect

6

that obtains in most encounters. My greatest chagrin in having met every day for two working weeks with Thomas Merton (on the collaboration with him of *A Thomas Merton Reader* [see Doubleday Image Books, 1974, revised edition]) was that I did not bring him the six-packs or cases of beer that I later learned—meaning the beer—was one of the great mundane passions of his life.

In any case, no pun intended, all this is simply to suggest that the saints are not above life and its earthly ingredients (and therefore not above and beyond us as well), but share what we share and love what we love, though we may as well grant to them a higher sense of order and priority. The saints in these essays are points of departure as well as points of arrival. They move in and out of the general theme of the ordinary person's experience in growing through age and wisdom toward God. It is Jesus Christ, of course, who is the ultimate locus of both mediation and meditation. The saints have no other purpose here than to lead us through Him to the unknown God. On a more human scale, I like to think of it all as a kind of Chaucerian pilgrimage in which we are not only likely but bound to meet the splendid variety of God's holy creation along the way. Some of these saints are the most popular in the litany, but none for the reason which is the central theme of this book. Teresa of Avila, Francis of Assisi, and Thomas More are among the most frequently selected of saints to write about. Monica and the Curé of Ars less so, while Jerome, Joseph, and John the Apostle are definitely eyebrow-raisers. An explanation for Job is clearly necessary, and Mary is the crown of the whole work.

How many saints indeed we might have gone on to discover as viable means to a longed-for goal? In the richness of souls that is the Church itself, the saints are legion. I am thinking of Saint Anthony, who survived temptation in the desert and lived to be one-hundred-five in the shade, and who was probably the true founder of Christian monasticism. I am thinking of Saint Camillus, who reformed and humanized the hospitals and nursing methods of his time; and gentle Hugh of Lincoln, the Carthusian, who also rose to occasions of anger when confronted wth the follies and injustices of his day; and Saint Jane Frances of Chantal and Saint Elizabeth Seton of our own time and country. And so many others, of course, with all those lovely Blesseds waiting in the wings — such candidates for canonization as Kateri Tekakwitha, Padre Pio, and Edith Stein. We are robed in the beauty of the saints.

In a very special sense, however, saints for the elderly are different. I mean they are different insofar as it is they — the elderly themselves — who have already entered what Evelyn and James Whitehead have so truly described as the "Sacrament of Aging":

> *It is only in the past century that the shape of a new stage of adult growth has appeared. Increased longevity has added several decades to adulthood, decades during which we may enjoy and contribute to life in a different mode. Retirement is not just a threshold of sickness and death; it can represent the transition into a new and important stage of adult maturity. Both this stage of maturity and one's passage into it invite a new ministerial response from the Church. . . . Through the sacrament of aging, and the communal and educational actions that support it, the mature person is helped to celebrate this stage of life: to move beyond despair or a compulsive living in the past into an appreciation of the present — beginning, in anticipation, the "uselessness" of an unending life with God.*

8

Saints for the elderly, you say? Indeed, they *are* the saints we look for. The elderly are people becoming saints in due season. If we do not see this, it is only because we are still too immature and too involved in our own preoccupations to have perceived the wholeness of the journey from beginning to end. The pilgrimage is no greater than the sum and substance of its pilgrims. With the spire of Canterbury in sight and grace a form of the divine luck, we shall all become saints in due season. Let us begin the journey with a prayer and call one another by first names.

1

Saint Monica

The Persistent Mother

What tigress is there that does not purr over her young
ones, and fawn upon them in tenderness?
—St. Augustine, *The City of God.*

---

*Monica was born of a Christian family, c. 331, at
Tagaste (Algeria) in North Africa. She married a
minor official of the region, Patricius (Patrick), a
man of less than wholly admirable character. She is
believed to have had three children by Patricius,
the eldest of whom was Augustine, later saint and
doctor of the Church. A virtuous mother of extraordinary strength and Christian fidelity, Monica's example and Augustine's own deep probings into religious thought and philosophy led to his conversion
on Easter eve, 387. Monica died that same year at
the port of Ostia, Italy, awaiting a return ship to
Africa. She was fifty-six. She is a patroness of married women. Her feast day is August 27.*

MONICA has to be one of the first saints with whom
anyone sixty-five or over can engage in that immediate sense of empathy which has to do mainly with
the raising of the unruly young. Ah, Monica, we may
now sigh virtuously from comfortable hindsight, what
trials of anguish all the sons of this world have put you
through in your lonely nights by the candlelit window,
or during all those endless days of wantonness and dis-
solution in the Carthages of our youth. But you were
lucky, Monica, to have had a son turn out the way Augustine did after his change of heart and habits. Luck,

of course, had nothing to do with it. Monica prayed mightily and mostly in the form of tears. A bishop she had consulted with, on the very problem of Augustine himself, gave her the reassurance that has since become famous: "It is not possible that the son of so many tears should be lost."

Monica is the saint of every mother—or, for that matter, of every father—who has wept for one's offspring or who, even tearless, has waited up half the night for their safe return home. It is both amazing and amusing how, at sixty-five and over, you begin to see the world from Monica's point of view: Of sons and daughters who act like compulsive little fools and the foolishness you have to tolerate from them in the compounded follies that an overindulgent world throws their way on the slightest provocation. There is implicit in all this, however, the hint that Monica herself might not have been the easiest kind of mother to get along with. You will have noted, perhaps, that the epigraph at the beginning of this chapter has characterized Monica, or any mother, as a tigress fawning upon her young with tenderness. How ironic that this inadvertent insight or perception should have come from Augustine himself. And yet Monica's love for Augustine was not a merely smothering kind of love, but a very keen and chastening demand that the young wanton should start preparing himself for better things and certainly, therefore, for a higher state of life.

It is no wonder that Augustine came at last to recognize the shocking contrast between the City of God and the City of Man; and that he came to recognize anything at all, as one of the greatest intellects the world has ever known, may be due in large part to the grace that Monica earned for him through her relentless prayers and copious tears. God knows, she was

11

good at it. She was a woman who forced the issue, and with her the issue was always a matter of Christian virtue and the total Christian commitment itself. One would have thought she had enough on her hands with her husband Patricius. His lackluster personality was no compensation for his ill-tempered nature, and it did not seem possible with this combination of traits that he would ever have any inclination to change his ways. However, Monica not only converted her husband, a year before he died, but *his* mother as well. Nothing much is known about the other two children of Patricius and Monica, the boy Navigius and the girl Perpetua, but they must have led fairly temperate and even exemplary lives—or else died young. It was, in any event, Augustine who caught the full force of Monica's irresistible piety.

The fact is, indeed, that one has almost to take Augustine himself hand in hand with Monica, for in a very real sense they deserved each other. He had his faults, God knows, though what God surely knew beyond this point has not been revealed to us; but it is certainly possible that Monica's eternal berating of Augustine may have pushed him to do the unseemly things he did in order to get back at her. It is the only way some children may have to punish their parents. If Monica had been a modern mother and Augustine a precocious child star, the push toward Hollywood would have been fierce and uncontested. Monica was overly ambitious for the glistening mark that she knew Augustine was bound to make in the world. He had all the makings in more ways than one, for he early learned bribery by stealing various items from his father's cellar and paying off his playmates for favors. He was bright and very clever and would no doubt get along in the world.

It does not require a crash course in depth psychology to realize that the interior tensions in Augustine were already made manifest, if not caused by, the outer abrasions daily evident between his own parents — the one so fiercely strong-willed and the other the pawn of his own characteristic weaknesses. It is in fact all the more likely that Augustine's father encouraged wantonness in his own son; and when Monica in turn all too frequently chided Augustine for his unseemly behavior, Patricius would tell her to stop such "woman's chatter." The domestic squabbling must have been very lively for a family in which two-fifths of its members would at length be recognized as saints by the Roman Catholic Church. This point about the family is extremely important, I think, because here was a fourth-century small family group that was in just as complete a state of disarray as those we see everywhere today in our own twentieth-century destruction of the Christian family.

It was Monica, however, who weathered the storm and who preserved whatever was left of the family; and what was left of the family, no less, was perhaps the most tremendous and salvific relationship between a mother and son in the whole history of Christendom—other than the one, of course, through which we have all been saved. In our own lifetime, in the days before the headier manifestations of women's liberation, so-called, it was often the strong wife and mother who held the family together. Our literature's most formidable example of such a woman may be seen in the Ma Joad of John Steinbeck's *The Grapes of Wrath* (1939), that great novel of the migration west from the Dust Bowl of Oklahoma in the Thirties. And yet Ma Joad herself had forebears in Willa Cather's Antonia Shimerda of *My Antonia* (1918), and especially in the authentic and historical characters of

13

such colonial women as Anne Hutchinson and the poet Anne Bradstreet. Again, in our own day, it is not untoward to think of Rose Kennedy, the mother of an assassinated president and matriarch of a notable American family, as a type of strong womanhood exemplified by Monica, the mother of Augustine.

Instead of the digression that all this may seem to be, it is important to take Monica out of antiquity and relate her to some kind of reality that we ourselves can recognize in our own time. I think that Monica was infinitely more than a merely nagging mother. She was formidable, to be sure, but also a thoroughly resourceful person on her own terms. She early acquired a vision of life that had recognized in the behavior of her son something other than the innocent high jinks of a carefree and spirited youth. This is a euphemistic way of saying that she saw him as a sinner. In riotous Carthage, he had taken to living with the young Christian concubine, Melania, who eventually bore him a son, Adeodatus (meaning "A Gift of God"), who in turn would later be baptized with Augustine himself on Easter eve in 387. Though tormented in his long relationship with Melania, Augustine displayed such traits of fidelity and responsibility to her and his son as would, in due time, hold him in good stead as a defender of the Faith and chief opponent of heresies to which he had himself once succumbed.

A further consideration, at this particular point, might be in order. There is no way of knowing, especially from a male point of view, the depths of anguish that mothers throughout the world must invariably experience as nurturers of the lives they have brought into existence. Aside from the relationship between a father and son, the closest that a man can come to this sense of anguish is in the resentful shock one might feel upon learning something untoward about someone we have always held—and still do hold—in the highest esteem. It was shocking to have learned, for instance, from Monica Furlong's biography, *Merton* (1980), that the young American undergraduate and future famed Cistercian monk may have fathered a child in England, and that he then abandoned the mother and child, both of whom were later reported to have been killed in a London air raid. I do not submit these remarks in any gratuitous or irrelevant fashion, for it is the only way I know to indicate to you the infinitely stronger feelings that Monica must have had toward the prolonged aberrations of her own son, Augustine, who, ironically enough, remained painfully loyal to his unwed wife and his son—two sons, therefore, who were brought into the Christian faith and fold through the insistent prayers and sorrowful tears of the beloved Monica. She was a saint, God knows, that anyone scarred by the many abrasions of the life experience itself must truly come to love and deeply understand.

It is a fact nonetheless that all we know of this great and sainted woman comes to us from Augustine himself, and there is perhaps no part of the *Confessions* more touching, more profound and searingly mystical, than the account he gives of Monica's death. It may also be said that in Monica and Augustine we have a witness to Christian death that was wholly realized centuries and centuries before the clinical-pastoral approach made popular by Elizabeth Kübler-Ross and other modern researchers. The morally chastening experience of Monica's death helps put the major attitudes of Augustine's life into proper perspective. Indeed, as the English journalist and historian Paul Johnson says, the *Confessions of St. Augustine* "is one of the few works of classical literature still read today because it centers around a personal relationship between the young, sinful Augustine and his pious Christian mother, Monica . . . and because it describes the author's efforts to overcome the sexual impulse" (*A History of Christianity*, Atheneum, New York, 1976). Despite popular interpretations of the *Confessions*, however, Johnson maintains there is no evidence that Augustine was ever the totally outrageous libertine he is commonly taken to have been, for even the relationship with a concubine was not unusual in those days.

In any event, infinitely more important than all this is Book Nine of *Confessions*, which reveals to us the extraordinary woman who was Monica. It is almost bizarre to suggest that death is an inhibiting factor which leaves us withdrawn and several times removed from the person in the throes of last days; but the impending, if not onrushing, death of Monica was the cause of some unparalleled conversations between a mother and son in such circumstances. There is nothing like these conversations in any literature I know. The implied third party in the conversations is, of course, God—to whom indeed the whole *Confessions* itself is addressed. We are lucky, if that is the word, which we mean perhaps as another term for grace, when we can witness the death of a parent with some degree of attendant love and devotion, despite all the anguish and sorrow that are also necessarily present. Candor and openness of heart are not always the most manifest bonds between parents and their offspring even when the children have grown into adults — or at least, that is, into the adult stage of life.

But in Monica and Augustine, the light years of estrangement and seemingly endless admonitions had already vanished in an instant. Both of them, sitting at a window that overlooked a courtyard garden in Ostia, opened their souls to one another. She had lived only to see Augustine become a Christian before she died. In the catharsis of her death, we know with Augustine that Monica had never been a merely nagging and distemperate mother, but that she was in fact a person who possessed an inexhaustible gift for the virtue of reconciliation. Augustine called it his mother's way, learned, as he said, in the school of her heart, where God himself was her secret teacher. When the brother, Navigius, expressed the hope that she would live long enough to die in her own country, beside her husband in the African earth they had both loved so much, Monica turned to Augustine and said, "See how he talks!" She told the two brothers that it did not matter where they buried her body, but asked them always to remember her at the altar of the Lord.

On the ninth day of her illness, Monica died. She was fifty-six and Augustine thirty-three. Here is how Augustine describes that moment in the preferred translation of R.S. Pine-Coffin, a Penguin Books paperback, in the twice-reprinted edition of 1975 (London): "I closed her eyes, and a great wave of sorrow surged into my heart. It would have overflowed in tears if I had not made a strong effort of will and stemmed the flow, so that the tears dried in my eyes. What a terrible struggle it was to hold them back!" Augustine pondered further the depth of his sorrow: "It can only have been because the wound was fresh, the wound I had received when our life together, which had been so precious and so dear to me, was suddenly cut off. I found comfort in the memory that as I did what I could for my mother in the last stages of her illness, she had caressed me and said that I was a good son to her. With great emotion she told me that she

17

could not remember ever having heard me speak a single hard or disrespectful word against her. And yet, O God who made us both, how could there be any comparison between the honor which I showed to her and the devoted service she had given me? It was because I was now bereft of all the comfort I had had from her that my soul was wounded and my life seemed shattered, for her life and mine had been as one.''

When the body of Monica was carried out for burial, Augustine said he came and went without a tear. He even thought to go to the local baths, for he had heard that "bathing rids the mind of anxiety," but there were no waters on earth that could wash away the bitter grief from Augustine's heart. He went to sleep and awoke refreshed and rested. It was only then, ironically, that the tears began to flow: "The tears which I had been holding back streamed down, and I let them flow as freely as they would, making of them a pillow for my heart." The sound of his weeping, he said, was for the ears of God alone: "And now, O Lord, I make you my confession in this book. Let any man read it who will. Let him understand it as he will. And if he finds that I sinned by weeping for my mother, even if only for a fraction of an hour, let him not mock at me. For this was the mother, now dead and hidden awhile from my sight, who had wept over me for many years so that I might live in your sight.'' Apparently, in those days, it was unseemly for a man to weep for one's mother, whereas in fact Augustine was only returning a fraction of the tears that she had long ago wept for him.

At least there was this between Monica and Augustine—that they had come to know one another as few are given to know the souls of other human beings in this life, let alone in that most painful of revelations

18

which may or may not transpire between parent and offspring. More often than not, of course, there is only a sense of stasis or impasse between parents and their immediate progeny. This is especially so, it seems, in the case of many Irish puritanical families repatriated in the New World locus of Yankee inhibition and deep-seated reticence. The plays of Eugene O'Neill are the American classics of this milieu, lacerated with anger and unregenerate madness, because they are so utterly devoid of those strengths and qualities which Monica had brought to a small, mostly non-Christian, family in North Africa centuries ago. She was pre-eminently the persistent mother and therefore a role-model in every way for the Christian stability of mind and purpose that the older person shall have hopefully acquired and maintained in the second half of life.

No older person has ever gained any sense of authority without due cost, and frequently at great cost, for it is a kind of authority that is based on the total expenditure of the life experience itself. Without either interfering in the lives of their adult children or inhibiting their freedom of self-determination, even in the likelihood that the young shall have surely made fools of themselves in the process, the older person should not surrender any sincere expression of those values which he or she may still hold dear and, what's more, may still consider usable. There are few instances imaginable, I think, in which an older person in the end will not prove to have been smarter (meaning wiser) than a younger one—that is, in lessons learned at great cost. It is unendurable that so many television commercials and portrayals in plays and movies so glibly promote images of the elderly that are nothing other than downright insulting and idiotic. Monica would not have put up with them for an instant; and if Augustine had been a Madison Avenue executive instead of one of the two greatest intellectuals ever produced by the Catholic Church (the other one being, of course, Saint Thomas Aquinas), let us hope that she would have whaled the hell out of him and shed not a tear for what she had done.

References and Suggested Readings

1. *A History of Christianity*, by Paul Johnson. Atheneum. New York, 1976.
2. *Confessions*, by Saint Augustine. Translated by R.S. Pine-Coffin. Penguin Books. London, 1975.
3. *An Augustine Reader*, edited, with an Introduction by John J. O'Meara. Image Books. Doubleday, New York, 1973.

2

Saint John Vianney (The Curé D'Ars)

The Understanding Listener

There is no great concurrence between learning and wisdom.

—Francis Bacon, *The Advancement of Learning* (1605)

John-Baptist Vianney was born on May 8, 1786, at Dardilly, near Lyons, in France, the son of a peasant farmer. At twenty, he was attracted to the priesthood and commenced his studies for ordination. An ecclesiastical student under the Abbé Balley, the young Vianney was nevertheless drafted through clerical error into the French army in 1809. To avoid military service, he went into hiding for fourteen months. A year later, in 1810, when Napoleon granted amnesty for all deserters, John Vianney returned home and shortly after was sent to the major seminary in Lyons. In 1818, he was assigned as parish priest to Arsen-Dombes, where he eventually became widely known for his pastoral and psychological gifts as a confessor. He died on August 4, 1859. He was canonized in 1925 and named patron of parish clergy by Pope Pius XI in 1929. His feast day is August 8.

IT WOULD seem at once that nothing could be duller than the life contained in the brief biographical sketch above of John-Baptist Vianney. Confessor extraordinary and saint withal, the outward events of his life appear to be as nondescript as the village to which he was first assigned as a parish priest. But there was something about this remarkable man, popularly known as the Curé d'Ars, that is presently in danger of slipping away from the Catholic consciousness in favor of the more flamboyant media types, such as rebellious theologians and second-rate clerical novelists. There has not been a first-rate biography of the Curé d'Ars, in English, for more than twenty years. And yet there is something quietly and persistently attractive about this saint. In the oppressive milieu of French provincialism in the nineteenth century, what was there in this seemingly very dull man that makes us want to remember him at all? I suggest at least two good reasons.

First, of course, there is always that unaccountable quality of quintessential holiness that tends to shock us right out of our shoes. Authentic spiritual integrity is the most shocking thing in the world. In an age in which the sex goddesses of the electronic media reign supreme in all the glittering capitals of the world, who is it that every now and then suddenly embarrasses us as we sit huddled in the dull blue glare of our domestic video screens? Mother Teresa. In the death-ridden streets of Calcutta or in the ruins of the bombed-out hospitals of West Beirut, the image of this holy woman clasping to her own thin and fragile form the body of yet another torn and wasted child, almost as big as Mother Teresa herself—this is something we cannot long abide to witness. True holiness is too much for us. The true holiness of John Vianney began as a rumor in the insufferably dull and venal small town of Ars.

Secondly, John Vianney was a born listener. Nobody listens today. Misdirected theologians, neo-Gnostic priest-journalists, liberated nuns in search of self-fulfillment, nobody wants to listen anymore. Everybody lectures and lays down the law to somebody else, and most of the time it is the person in legitimate authority who is taking all the gaff from people who refuse to listen in the first place. Listening well is one of the great lost virtues of our time. On the other hand, it was in fact John Vianney himself who had all but listened his way to sainthood. He ended up listening to the troubles of thousands of people.

I must confess, at this point, that the kindest individuals I know have always been those who have listened long and creatively to the problems of others. It is perfectly natural, I think, that folks over sixty-five—or approaching that age of wisdom which is located generally in the second half of life—should have long since become very good listeners. After all, we have been listening longer than anyone else. We know from common experience that the young do not listen too well. They absorb like crazy, to be sure, but they are not too great on listening up close. This accounts for the curious phenomenon that when the young want somebody else to listen to *them*, they invariably go to a veteran listener — some genial but long-suffering aunt or uncle or grandparent. The Curé of Ars was the best priest-listener in the business.

The fact remains, however, that more and more priests coming out of all those sociological seminars and crash psychology programs are listening less and less these days. The Curé of Ars would have had none of that and, what's more, he wouldn't have understood any of it. The two most commonly known facts about John Vianney are: (1) that he had trouble with his Latin studies; and (2) that he was very good at hearing confessions. So much has been made of his deficiency in scholastic endeavors that the popular impression has been that he wasn't—well, you know, too bright. It is true, perhaps, academically speaking, that the head of the class would have been a somewhat strange seating arrangement for the young seminarian; but it is also true that John Vianney was nevertheless a highly intelligent and qualified candidate for the priesthood. Conditions in the France of that time were not too conducive to studies for the priesthood. In the period from 1806 to 1815, the young seminarian missed some fourteen months of instruction while in hiding from the military authorities. In the end, all the same, it was as much the goodwill of his superiors as it was Vianney's own scholastic qualifications, or lack of them, which saw him at last through ordination. What everyone would come to realize later, however, is that he had other gifts and attributes which were not in any way derived from the pedagogy of the classroom.

All he understood, of course, was human nature itself. As that unlikely corroborator of the Abbé Vianney's gifts of insight, Ralph Waldo Emerson, wrote in his *Journals* one late summer day in 1842: "All persons are puzzles until at last we find in some word or act the key to the man, to the woman; straightway all their past words and actions lie in light before us" (*The Heart of Emerson's Journals*, edited by Bliss Perry, Houghton Mifflin Company, Boston, 1926). The Curé of Ars was indeed unusually struck with deep insights into the souls of men and women. It is not uncommon in the experience of the average person to have known someone like that at one time or another—and, again, not uncommonly—from rural or even very remote areas. Such a person was invariably unschooled in formal matters, but full of a deep and quiet wisdom of the heart. People in the second half of life, I think, ought to have a wholesome and natural respect for a man like John Vianney, because, among

24

other reasons we shall soon consider, he had acquired his insights into human nature long before he had reached his old age. In other words, he was wise before he was old.

Having said this, however, the myth of the Curé of Ars persists. Bishop Norbert F. Gaughan, probably the most literate member of the U.S. hierarchy since Cardinal John J. Wright, wrote in a column for *Our Sunday Visitor* newspaper (August 1, 1982) that John Vianney was a type of student who had to work extremely hard at his studies: "Anything he gained in the way of knowledge had to be done by hard work and long hours of study. But his sanctity was not then a triumph of holiness over stupidity. He understood that the priesthood called for more than just knowing Latin; it demanded hard work. He proved it too. Anyone who spent as much as eighteen or more hours a day in the confessional had to work hard." We must notice as well, Bishop Gaughan continues, "what John Vianney did as a pastor," which, again, was simply and infinitely more than any typical suburban pastor does today. "The modern priest may have a harder job description than even John Vianney had," but I am less optimistic than is Bishop Gaughan in presuming that more than a very few have done their jobs half so well.

The point is, of course, that John Vianney had pastoral expertise of a kind not usually recognized by the dispensers of academic awards and honors. It is also important that we should have at least some glancing knowledge of the social context in which the Curé of Ars worked. This is a fancy way of saying that an isolated French village in the nineteenth century was not highly regarded as a thriving source of spiritual refreshment and renewal. The whole drama of Georges

Bernanos' classic novel, *Journal d'un Curé de Campagne* (1935), is based on the spiritual depletion of a type of French provincial life so pervasive as to cause the young curate to record its effect almost at once in his diary: "My parish is bored stiff; no other word for it. Like so many others! We can see them being eaten up by boredom, and we can't do anything about it. Some day perhaps we shall catch it ourselves—become aware of the cancerous growth within us. You can keep going a long time with that in you" (*The Diary of a Country Priest*, by Georges Bernanos, translated from the French by Pamela Morris, Image Books, Doubleday and Company, New York, 1974).

The boredom, the curate continues, was like dust: "You go about and never notice, you breathe it in, you eat and drink it. It is sifted so fine, it doesn't even grit on your teeth. But stand still for an instant and there it is, coating your face and hands. To shake off this drizzle of ashes you must be forever on the go. And so people are always 'on the go.' Perhaps the answer would be that the world has long been familiar with boredom, that such is the true condition of man." The indictment is so devastating—moreso, one may possibly argue, than anything envisioned in the similarly dusty wasteland of the poet T.S. Eliot — that the young priest wonders whether "a man has ever before experienced this contagion, this leprosy of boredom: an aborted despair, a shameful form of despair in some way like the fermentation of a Christianity in decay."

The elderly know what is meant by a state of boredom so penetrating and universal that it all but crushes the human spirit. And yet, despite the fact that the elderly have been implicitly declared a non-people in this country and are daily insulted by both benign

26

and pernicious neglect, and who are also asked to live on pittances, it is probably the unhappy truth that nothing so much contributes to a sense of despair in the elderly as their all-too-frequent refusal to come to terms with the fact and irreversible reality of aging itself. Despair is the ultimate denial of self-acceptance. Gerontology, or the study of aging, at best, cannot abolish old age, as such, but only make it happen later.

What has all this to do with the young John Vianney dispatched to the miserable parish of Ars-en-Dombes, in 1818, and who was destined to remain there for some forty years until his death in 1859? Certainly, the young priest was entering an atmosphere such as that experienced by the priest in the novel by Georges Bernanos, "a shameful form of despair in some way like the fermentation of a Christianity in decay." Still, it was in such a setting as this that the Abbé Vianney revitalized and literally saved the lives of tens of thousands of people who sought him out, as a confessor and spiritual director, in a neglected village gone to seed and reduced to the dust of spiritual desolation. Leave it to the great English essayist G. K. Chesterton to have recognized in the Curé of Ars someone who was not only challenging but possibly aggravating as well. It was typical of Chesterton also to have said of the Curé of Ars that there was "nothing apologetic about his apologetics." I cannot think of anything that would more endear such a saint to the elderly than just that, when, at least past age sixty-five, most of us have long since given up our coy and groveling apologies like a bad habit.

It would satisfy a nice and orderly sense of the law of compensation to say that John Vianney at length lived out his life—that is, until the time of his death at seventy-three—in the peace and spiritual tranquillity which he so thoroughly deserved. But that is not the way it was, as it is not the way with many who reach the seventh and eighth decades of their lives, for the Abbe Vianney was frequently tormented with both spiritual doubts and visitations from an adversary he took to be Satan himself, and which may have been the psychological product of a totally exhausted man. One puts it in this tentative manner if only to allow for our increase in knowledge about these matters since the time of John Vianney, while also allowing for the perhaps still greater perceptions of the aging confessor himself into areas of our spiritual realities. Certainly, too, there was the business of the three or four attempted "flights" of the Curé of Ars from his pastoral commitments to the solitude and anonymity of the monastery. In each instance, however, he was persuaded to return to the village of Ars and resume his duties to the end.

God knows, if his superiors seemed not to, John Vianney could have used an occasional retreat to the monastery. He had been worked beyond endurance, worked down and out, as it were, like the itinerant poor relation who had come home to die in Robert Frost's famous poem, "The Death of the Hired Man." The figure for such a reference does not seem to me entirely out of place. I have seen the likes of those hard-working men and women who once sparsely peopled the northern farmlands of New England. I mean only to suggest that in my grandparents especially, an Aroostook potato farmer and his taciturn but quietly smiling wife, I had some slight but very real knowledge of the French Canadian rural and village life which, until only a few decades ago, must have been something like the milieu that the Abbé Vianney had known in the countryside of Ars-en-Dombes. If it was the destiny of the peasants to work the land, however, and the business of the townspeople to ply the trades of the village, it was left to the Curé of Ars to carry the still greater burdens of the spirit—which is to say, of course, all the joys and the sorrows and the salvation of souls under his loving and scrutinous care.

Such a task would have to take its toll from any man. It exacted a dear and particularly harsh toll from John Vianney. There is a paragraph from Henri Gheon's *Secrets of the Saints* (Translated by F.J. Sheed. Sheed and Ward, New York, 1949), a classic in its English translation of the Forties and now long out of print, which I reproduce here for its cogent summation of that which best reveals to us, I think, the quintessential nature and character of the saint: "The confessional, the answering of letters, the tricks of Satan, toothache and gastric pains, the maddening pricks of the hair shirt, want of food and sleep: add to that doubts as to his vocation and a pressing feeling of his unworthiness—for we must put all these things together, since all were pressing on him at once—did ever man have so many crosses? We are driven to say that his efforts at flight were less the work of the Evil Spirit than the sheer weariness of the flesh. M. Vianney was a poor man with a poor body—and his poor body could hold out no longer. A few years later came a villainous cough to rack him and to keep him from sleep even when the devil had given him up as a bad job."

The devil's bad job is for the rest of us an enduring source of inspiration. We may very well wonder where such devotion to the priesthood exists today. I have never, in all my life as a suburban parishioner, seen a priest so much as mow the front lawn of the rectory, pick up the empty beer cans that the CYO teenagers

29

discard outside the church hall, or in winter shovel the snow from the walkways and front steps of the church entrance itself. For some reason that has never been clear to me, American priests of the urban and sub-urban variety are not supposed to soil their hands or to suffer them the unseemly possibility of raising an occasional callus. Let it be known that I speak in this manner for all well-seasoned curmudgeons and for many a forthright lady who can still wield a mean walking stick flush in the face of nonsense and folly. We do not suffer fools gladly. We do not look fawningly upon those of the ordained who, fresh from the seminaries, now and then lecture us on received lessons of life they have got out of textbooks and sessions in group psychology. It is enough that we should have to listen to bad sermons in cold churches, with the PA system left turned down, because, after all, why should it ever occur to the clergy that perhaps a good third of the congregation may be slightly hard of hearing? I realize this may be a blessing in disguise, but just for the record one ought to hear what the rascals are saying.

It is said that the preaching of the Curé of Ars was straightforward and plain. He nevertheless knew how to explicate the Gospel, which, of course, is something that the average American priest has never learned to do. There had to be something of the evangelical imperative of John Vianney. One mentions this element in him because, since it is now possible for the Roman Catholic to see and hear evangelical preaching on television and radio almost any day or night of the week, it has become obvious to us all that your basic Baptist preacher, for example, can explicate Gospel text almost endlessly and from any given chapter and verse. What made Abbé Vianney different from all other preachers of the Gospel, however, was that he also extended it to the applied psychology of the confessional. He was, in the nineteenth century, already light years ahead of the rote confessions and numbers game that we used to play like Russian roulette in our youth.

I remember, on Saturday afternoons, sitting with other little hardened sinners in straight-backed wooden pews which gradually and inevitably displaced their sniveling occupants, one at a time, directly in front of the confessonal curtain. Almost every Catholic can probably look back and tell you his or her exclusive confessional horror story, or at least one that is still mildly shocking, but which did not result in a total loss of faith and may have even increased it, without our knowing exactly why, over the ensuing years into adulthood. Such stories range from Frank O'Connor's superb irish classic, "First Confession," to the sardonic and bitter disillusionments of the young Mary McCarthy in *Memories of a Catholic Girlhood*—the one a recoverable experience and the other a derangement of faith that has lasted a lifetime. As a young man, too, I used to see the old women going to confession in a downtown shrine for commuters and shoppers in Boston, and I was always mystified as to why they stayed inside the confessional for seemingly interminable periods of time. What sins could they possibly have had to confess that were as bad as all that?

The Curé of Ars would have known that these were, by and large, essentially lonely souls in search of human and, if possible, divine contact at a stage of life when such matters begin to encroach themselves upon us with a new and quietly urgent sense of resolution. John Vianney was preeminently the priest of confession. However, confession was indeed too important a matter to have been so long trivialized with our endless accountings for childish peccadillos by the numbers. The Second Vatican Council recognized this situation, I think, and then proceeded to reduce the sacrament to a state of disarray and confusion. It was probaby, next to the Mass itself, the most ineptly renewed of the Church's sacraments. And yet there is some benefit to be derived from less frequent routine confessions, even though they may impart to us a minimal sense of spiritual consolation. Certainly, at an older age, when our opportunities for a life of hedonism have been critically reduced and we have suddenly acquired a largeness of humor and spirit that we never knew we had, then the confessional becomes of little pragmatic use to us. Do penance, yes, but without becoming morbidly penitential—as if wallowing in the lugubrious regrets of a misspent life were going to do you any good at all.

I think it is important to take particular note of the brief biographical sketch of John-Baptist Vianney, at the beginning of this essay, which states that the saint was named by Pope Pius XI, in 1929, as patron of parish clergy. He was a model of the priesthood that is almost benignly scorned today. But it was G.K. Chesterton who, in the short essay he wrote as an epilogue to the first English edition of Henri Gheon's *The Secret of the Curé d'Ars*, recognized in the saint the ultimate challenge to our times. He said of John Vianney that he was not only challenging, he was aggravating: "He was a walking contradiction; he cut across the whole trend of his time at right angles, quite content to know that the angle was right."

In the end, he has also taught us that what we often mistake as cantankerousness in the elderly is simply the effect of a strong-willed urge to go on living in such light of the last days as may still be left to each of us.

References and Suggested Readings

1. *The Heart of Emerson's Journals*, edited by Bliss Perry. Hougton Mifflin Company. Boston, 1926.
2. *The Diary of a Country Priest*, by Georges Bernanos. Translated by Pamela Morris. Image Books. Doubleday and Company. New York, 1974
3. *Secrets of the Saints*, by Henri Gheon. Translated by F. J. Sheed. Sheed and Ward. New York, 1949.

3

Saint Teresa of Avila

Woman of the Divine Realities

The eternal feminine draws us upward.
—J. W. Goethe, *Faust II* 1832)

Teresa of Avila was born at Avila in Castile, Spain, on March 28, 1515. She was the daughter of the Castilian nobleman Don Alonso Sanchez de Cepeda and his second wife, Doña Beatriz de Ahumeda. At sixteen, Teresa was sent as a student to the Augustinian convent at Avila, but only a year later was forced to leave the convent school because of illness. She then became seriously interested in the religious life and decided, against her father's initial wishes, to join the Carmelites at Avila in 1536. She was in fact professed the following year, but left in 1538, again for reasons of ill health. Her religious experiences continued to intensify, however, and after a prolonged and difficult period she founded her first monastery for nuns, St. Joseph Convent at Avila, whose members sought to lead a more ordered spiritual life than that provided by the easy and relaxed style of the convents of the period. It was in the founding of her second monastery that Teresa met the young friar, John Yepes, later known to the world as St. John of the Cross. Teresa died in Alba de Tormes on October 4, 1582. She was canonized in 1622 by Pope Gregory XV and declared a doctor of the Church in 1970 by Pope Paul VI. Her feast day is October 15.

SAINT TERESA of Avila may not at first seem quite a proper saint for people in the second half of life. She was so given to ills of the flesh and torments of the spirit that some might consider her a depressing figure at best. It may even come as a startling implication to say that any given saint at any given time of life could be considered more or less improper for anyone; but as long as we live, no doubt, our quirky natures and passionate preferences, as the poet Robert Frost used to say, will prevail. For instance, I think it would be rather unlikely in one's mature or advanced old age to become enamored of a gung-ho saint like Joan of Arc, who is preeminently the saint of one's youth. If the Maid of Orléans had struck a mortal blow to your heart, when you were still especially young, as she did, say with the mind and heart of the Boston-born young man who would later become Cardinal John J. Wright, it was enough to last a lifetime. But I still think that Joan was a saint for romantics, and I have never been able to get out of my head the notion of George Bernard Shaw's that she was the first Protestant saint. In any case, I think people who leap suddenly into the air, with swords in their hands, must remain rather large bores to elderly folk in search of peace and quiet.

More seriously, though, what's likely to scare one off from a woman like Teresa of Avila is that undefined something which has to do with all those foreboding stages of mysticism contained in those imposing volumes of her spiritual writings that are in themselves perhaps too difficult and esoteric for most people to read even in part, let alone straight through. Too much holiness, as Evelyn and James Whitehead earlier suggested, may be hazardous to your health. But I would like in turn to suggest as well that Teresa was a glorious woman for all that; and since I am, like you, a pilgrim on the downslope of the mountain, I want to tell you in my own curious and admittedly subjective way why Saint Teresa of Avila would make an incomparable traveling companion. She knew the territory, she knew the roads, and at least on one occasion dared to tell God to stop shoving.

To begin with, however, there were all those medical problems. In the annals of hagiography, there are few saints or candidates for sainthood who have had medical problems the way Teresa of Avila had medical problems. We usually think of saints as ethereal beings that float through life on velleities of inspiration which are automatically supplied to them from divine and therefore very remote sources. For instance, we prefer to think that Thérèse of Lisieux, also a Carmelite, was indeed the Little Flower, all pure and pink and gathering roses, that we see pictured on religious cards with those perceived pieties printed on the reverse side. Do you mind if I tell you that I once wrote a published poem about this, more specifically about the standard photograph of the saint that was distributed by the sisters of her Carmelite convent, but which was also retouched and enhanced over the objections of a Father Etienne Robo, a French-born priest and contemporary of Thérèse, who had made some original photographs of the saint? Sanctity, in its most attractive outlines, is clearly what the world prefers. But of course the pristine and terrible truth is that Thérèse of the Child Jesus suffered dreadfully from tuberculosis at a time when medical science was unable to prolong her life beyond the age of twenty-four.

Teresa of Avila had been only one year younger than that, as a matter of fact, when she began to hear voices and experience visions, while, at the same time, suffering her strangely recurring illnesses. As an amateur in these matters and susceptible to some

36

of the theories of the psychiatrist Carl Gustav Jung, I have the notion that Teresa was also at this time undergoing an interior turbulence which was thrusting her onward to that psychic climax of "individuation" which would henceforth determine the character and career of the saint once and for all. This may have accounted for some of her medical problems, but probably left still more of them unexplained and perhaps even unexplainable. As a child of the sixteenth century, she could not have always recognized her difficulties as specifically known medical problems in the first place, and therefore attributed them to supernatural, often demonic, causes. So it would have been little wonder at all, in any case, that Teresa should have made the slightest sense from the continuing onslaught of her various maladies.

At the Carmelite monastery of the Incarnation, Teresa was stricken to such an extent that her father, Don Alonso decided to take his daughter to Becedas, a small town about fifty miles southwest of Avila, for what we must now shudder to think of as the cure. In his admirable translation of the *Life* or autobiography of St. Teresa of Avila (also known as the Book of Her Life), Kieran Kavanaugh, O.C.D., refers to this "cure" episode as having been administered from the hands of a "quack." Quack, I think, is not quite the term. It too much implies a kind of outrageous deviation from already enlightened treatment, but the established treatment of the time existed only in the form of a more solemn order of quackery. The long-robed Castilian physicians could not do much more than take pulse, examine urine, and then hold involved consultations which at length failed to explain anything at all. It was only in degree that worse than this was the "method" of the *curandera*, or lay-healer, in

37

this instance a woman in Becedas who was believed to have had some successes with hopeless cases.

If the case of Teresa was not hopeless (only because of her own strength of will and belief in the restorative powers of heaven), it was certainly desperate enough. The *curandera* did not practice her trade in the winter, since fresh herbs were then unavailable, so Teresa had to wait until spring for any treatment at all. The herbs the lay-healer gathered were supposed to act as vomitives and purgatives to shock and flush out the body—and, God knows, whatever else these herbs may have done, they did just that. This much having failed, however, the *curandera* would then resort to a sort of medical exorcism and administer to the unfortunate patient only such materials as could be derived from the rejuvenating forces of the earth itself; diced toes of spring frogs; powder from the pulverized wings of the first flies of spring; and the fresh excreta of skin-shedding snakes. The cure was not only worse than the disease, according to the familiar equation, but it almost killed Teresa in the bargain. Some bargain, some cure.

One of the most touching parts of the autobiography (see Chapter Five) has to do with Teresa's three-month sojourn "at that place" (Becedas), as she called it, and which she finally left with so overwhelming a sense of spiritual sadness that she could find no rest either by night or by day. If twentieth-century medical scientists could have examined Teresa, what would they have found? I am familiar with only one essay that has attempted to consider this question in any detail whatsoever, and it is by René Fülop-Miller in *The Saints That Moved the World,* published in 1945 by Thomas Y. Crowell, long a favorite book of mine. Fülop-Miller believes that modern science would have summarized her symptoms about as follows: "Her convulsions were tonic contractions: the rigidity of her muscles was a form of muscular tetanization; the choking sensation, which made it so difficult for her to swallow, was a globus *hystericus*; her unendurable pain is indicative of hyperesthesia; her frequent fainting spells were due to nervous disorders in the circulatory system"; and it simply goes on like that, suggesting at last a treatment that "would consist of a cold-water cure with Luminal and Dilantin as drugs and possibly psychoanalysis." The wonder is, of course, how Teresa had managed to penetrate all this pathology and still achieve a life of active reform, contemplative genius, and something very close to a state of spiritual perfection.

I have taken pains to go on with these matters about Teresa's physical condition only because we are so likely, in our own enlightened times, to presume that now we know so much better than all that; and yet we often allow our nursing homes to degenerate into medically scandalous institutions, and in general treat the elderly and the infirm with shameful disregard. To some in the early stages of old age, the symptoms and ailments of Teresa will have seemed like a horror story; but to others already there, the distressful afflictions of Teresa are in many cases a too familiar litany. We can only wish that these latter souls will also have found even the slightest portion of the spiritual resources that were granted to Teresa in order to help her bear the sometimes terrible consequences of human existence.

What Teresa possessed, of course, was an almost elemental force of spirit. Extinguish her spirit, and she would have died early and unknown. I call it a certain nobility of soul. It is a quality that is frequently present in people who have led simple and very hard lives, though Teresa herself was an intensely complex person. When present in women especially, the quality of nobility of soul is made manifest to us in an almost luminous yet thoroughly substantial way. It is not a characteristic of the past only, for we have surely recognized this nobility of the human spirit in the late Dorothy Day, for example, and certainly in Mother Teresa of Calcutta. Edith Stein had nobility of soul. Also a Carmelite nun, known in religion as Benedicta of the Cross, Edith Stein was gifted with formidable powers of intellect; and more than anyone else in modern times, I think, she has in this and other respects maintained the Teresian continuity.

For instance, where now it is believed that Teresa of Avila was of partly Jewish heritage, Edith Stein of course was wholly a Jew and put to death, on that account alone, by her Nazi captors at Auschwitz, Germany, in 1942. Just as Teresa had experienced some early but nevertheless maturing influences on her spiritual and philosophical formation, such as the curious mystical instructions of the Franciscan monk Francisco de Osuna, Edith Stein became a follower of Edward Husserl, the phenomenologist, whose esoteric teachings were also an extremely important factor in the formation of the student Karol Wojtyla, who, of course, later became Pope John Paul II. Edith Stein was one of the most beautiful souls of our time, and anyone interested in Teresa of Avila should also be interested in this remarkable convert and contemplative. We should pray day and night for her canonization. One of her great works, by the way, is *The Science of the Cross* (1960), a study of Teresa's great collaborator in Carmelite spirituality, St. John of the Cross himself. The scarcity of books by and about her, in good English translations, is a scandal to whatever may be left of Catholic publishing both in this country and in England.

When I said earlier that an advanced spiritual presence in women takes on a luminous but inherently substantial aspect, I meant in a way which holds and even binds the most divine intuitions to the earthly realities of our human existence. A few years ago, there was a book published by Knopf under the simple title *Anna* (1975), which did not receive much attention in the book reviewing press, but which I still can't forget for the nobility it conveyed to me of the human spirit under duress. The main character in this true story has become lodged in my mind as the secular saint, Anna of Haugestvolden, a simple Norwegian woman who, in this enlightened twentieth century of ours, had literally been sold by her drunken husband into lifelong bondage as a common laborer on a mountain wilderness farm. The miracle of Anna is not only that she survived this strictly male-imposed bondage and thorough dehumanization—which, at one point, found her stretched on the earth and her fingers dug into the ground with almost paralyzing desperation—but that she also transcended all this to discover a spiritual dimension and presence of God that she had not heretofore known. Anna was the earth, and she was its sadness and its tragedy and also its ultimate triumph. Her eyes were sourced, I like to think, in that ineffable beauty which we shall never see reflected in what Robert Frost once called, in a favorite poem, the picture queens of Hollywood. She had seen all there was to see and her hands had done all the work there was to do. There was nothing more that she could do; and so, in her eighties, Anna died serenely and at peace even with those who had so cruelly oppressed her.

41

I have gone on at length about Anna of Haugestvolden because her strength of spirit was similar to
Teresa's, and I do not think it is either untoward or in-
appropriate to compare the social and cultural circumstances which each of them had to transcend in order to become what their spiritual destinies demanded
they should become — in short, saints of one kind or
another.

Teresa's transcendence over her environment was
more complex than Anna's, but she was by no means
the ultimate female religious liberator some fashion-
ably feminist writers have unaccountably taken her to
be. More misapplied than even this, however, are
some of the Freudian interpretations that are current-
ly all the rage in so-called psychobiography and other
arbitrary analyses of prominent people no longer
around to defend themselves against the excesses of
both academic ignorance and arrogance.

In this regard, I want to cite in particular the ex-
travagant nonsense of a recent Freudian analysis of
the saint, by an academic feminist writer, moreover,
who has given her essay the all but predictable title "A
Psycho-Spiritual History of Teresa of Avila." Imagine
trying to explain Teresa's conversion (meaning her
commitment to the religious life) in strictly Freudian
terms. Amusing, too, if we were not so flagrantly
wrongheaded, is the attempt to explain away Teresa's
medical ailments as a psychotic state of atonement for
her mother's childbearing years and general debilita-
tion, whatever that means, though the author curiously
fails to mention the fact that what may have led to the
debilitations of Doña Beatriz de Ahumeda was her
heavy addiction to the serialized novels about the
"darkly beautiful" knight, Amadis of Gaul, satirized
by Cervantes in the great Spanish classic *Don Quix-*

ote. It is equally silly to presume, I think, as the feminist author chooses to presume, that Teresa's body had become sexually "neutered" at age forty—again, presumably, the fate of all female human bodies at that ominous age, and so on.

One of the most serious affronts to the elderly—and, indeed, to many other people who are little more than halfway there—is to presume that the sexual presence or aura of a person ceases to function when genital activity itself goes into decline. I have always sensed a most delightful and abiding sexual relationship in talking with women well past their most provocative years, so to speak, and also with women whose various states of life are not given to sexual activity for perfectly good reasons having wholly to do with other kinds of personal commitment. There is no mistaking the feminine presence in everything written by Teresa of Avila, in all three volumes of the *Works* generally available and in the two volumes of the incomparable *Letters*. It is at least arguable, in my opinion, that the most exquisite single volume of mystical theology ever written is Teresa's *The Interior Castle*, and yet all the more astonishing when one realizes that this great spiritual classic was composed in probably no more than two months of Teresa's actual working time—time that had to be divided and shared with her numerous administrative duties as well. As for Teresa's "neutered" sexual identity, someone ought to tell our feminist expert that in Spain itself you can refer to "La Madre" (The Mother) and everyone will know that you mean Teresa de Cepeda.

It nevertheless remains a fact that in the best possible sense Teresa was indeed a notable figure as far as women's rights were concerned. This in itself is not to take on the follies and delusions of the modern feminists, but simply to acknowledge the perpetual struggle that Teresa had to wage against a benighted and sometimes malicious use of ecclesiastical authority. Feminists would say that she had to struggle against male authority, as such, and then conveniently forget that the best friends and associates she had were men. In any event, the elderly will admire her intelligent assertiveness, for few are more assertive of their rights, legal and moral, than the class of older citizens now awakening to the fact that they have been slightly put upon. They have to fight for their rights, because nobody else will. They often feel as weary and defeated as did Teresa herself, who, at sixty-three, with four more years to live, could say of herself that she was "good for very little now, very old and weary," and then add in typically Teresian tones: "Yet my desires are still vigorous." It was at this time that a newly appointed papal nuncio, prejudiced against the reforming activity of the Discalced Carmelites, said of Teresa: "She is a disobedient, contumacious woman, who promulgates pernicious doctrines under the pretense of devotion, who left her cloister against the orders of her superiors, who is ambitious and teaches theology as though she were a doctor of the Church, in contempt of the teachings of Saint Paul who commanded women not to teach." Assuming an air of affected irony, Teresa herself reported these charges to Philip II, King of Spain, who in turn courteously ignored the ridiculous allegations and sanctioned her cause. So, of course, do we.

In that book of Teresa's which best exemplifies her profound and motherly solicitude for souls under her care, the great *Way of Perfection*, she touches on the problem of prayer in old age and seems to suggest that it may be a time in which we are more likely to practice vocal prayer than mental prayer—if, indeed, we had ever practiced mental prayer at all. Creatures of lifelong habits, we shall not suddenly abandon in our advanced years what we have been accustomed to most of our lives. Some are tuned to vocal prayer and some to mental prayer and the spiritual delights beyond. Teresa knew that most of us do not get much further along than this basic first level of the prayer life, and yet she is exquisitely sensitive to that and does not demean us for having failed to reach the greater heights achieved by true contemplatives:

"I know an elderly person," she writes, "who lives a good life, is penitential and an excellent servant of God, who has spent many hours for many years in vocal prayer, but in mental prayer she's helpless; the most she can do is go slowly in reciting the vocal prayers. There are a number of other persons of this kind. If humility is present, I don't believe they will be any worse off in the end, but will be very much the equals of those who receive many delights; and in a way they will be more secure, for we [meaning, of course, the more advanced] do not know if the delights are from God or from the devil." As for the rest of us, "There is nothing to fear; don't be afraid that you will fail to reach the perfection of those who are very contemplative" (*The Collected Works of St. Teresa of Avila,* Vol. II, translated by Kieran Kavanaugh, O.C.D., and Otilio Rodriguez, O.C.D., ICS Publications, Washington, D.C., 1976). At a well-advancing age, in fact, one ought to avoid scrupulosity of any kind. Like constipation, it really isn't going to do you any good. The greatest prayer is to leave oneself open to the mercy of God.

It is a blunt reality, of course, that we cannot always clearly understand just what is meant by the mercy of God; and this seems all the more likely, I think, when the cumulative afflictions of the years are not likely to be accepted as the received mercies or casual endearments of the Lord. (For instance, when Mother Teresa of Calcutta told a patient in her spiritual care that her suffering was but the kiss of Jesus, the patient replied, "Mother Teresa, please tell Jesus to stop kissing me.")

And when Teresa of Avila herself was the aging *madre*, she went by mule cart on countless visitations to her older foundations and even sought to establish—and did establish—a last convent at Burgos to the greater glory of her beloved Saint Joseph.

The story is well-known, but always worth retelling, that in attempting to wade across the River Arlanzon with her nuns, Teresa slipped on a rock and was swept down the river. On recovering herself, she said: "Oh, Lord, why do you put such difficulties in our way?" The Lord, appearing over the water to her, replied: "It is thus I treat my friends." And she in turn, playing one-upmanship with the Second Person of the Blessed Trinity, said: "Ah, my Lord, that is why you have so few of them."

Teresa went on from Burgos to the convent at Alba de Tormes, and that would prove to be her final such visitation. In Alba, she suffered a hemorrhaging of the lungs from which she would not recover. She had indeed suffered many "little deaths" before, but she knew at last that this was the great and ultimate moment.

Though she had written ecstatic poems to death as a mystical experience, I love our mother Teresa for this lovely and very simple line of prose: "What happiness to think that we are not going to a strange country, but to our own."

References and Suggested Readings

1. *The Collected Works of St. Teresa of Avila.* Vols. I, II. Translated by Kieran Kavanaugh, O.C.D. and Otilio Rodriguez, O.C.D. ICS Publications. Institute of Carmelite Studies, Washington, D.C., 1976.
2. *The Saints That Moved the World,* by René Fülop-Miller. Thomas Y. Crowell, New York, 1945.
3. *The Letters of Saint Teresa of Jesus.* Translated and edited by E. Allison Peers. The Newman Press, Westminster, Md., 1950.
4. *Faith According to St. John of the Cross,* by Karol Wojtyla. Translated by Jordan Aumann, O.P. Ignatius Press, San Francisco, 1981.
5. *Ways to Know God,* by Sister Teresia Benedicta of the Cross, O.C.D. (Edith Stein). With a biographical essay by Sister Josephine Koeppel, O.C.D. An Edith Stein Guild Publication © The Thomist, Washington, D.C., 1946.

4
Saint Jerome

The Pleasures of Irascibility

He who is of a calm and carefree nature will but lightly feel
the pressures of old age; whereas to anyone of a contrary disposition, youth and age are equally burdensome.

—Plato, *The Republic*

---

*Jerome was born at Strido in Dalmatia in about
the year 342. He was known as Eusebius Hieronymus Sophronius and remained unbaptized for
more than twenty years. He studied in Rome and
became proficient in Latin, Greek, and classical
studies. He was baptized by Pope Liberius in 360,
and a decade later went to Syria and lived among
the desert hermits near Antioch. Here he learned
Hebrew, lived under a regimen of prayer and fast-
ing, and wrote the life of Saint Paul of Thebes. He
then studied Scripture in Constantinople with St.
Gregory Nazianzen and thus became involved in
the field of scholarship for which he is still known
today. After his ordination in Antioch, he declined
to exercise his priestly office on the grounds that it
was incompatible with his vocation as a scholar. In
Rome, from 382 to 385, he served as secretary to
Pope Damasus and was directed by him to revise
the Latin version of the New Testament. On the
death of the pope, Jerome returned to the East, settled in Bethlehem with a community of followers
and disciples, and flourished in both biblical scholarship and controversy for the rest of his life. He
died at Bethlehem in 420, after a prolonged illness,
on September 30, now observed as his feast day.*

IT BEGINS with irascibility, though hardly in a joyful

manner, for what is to become of anyone born with a name like Eusebius Hieronymus Sophronius? And then to say, as do practically all the dictionaries of saints you can lay your hands on, to say that he (Jerome) was born at a place called Strido, near Aquileia, in Dalmatia, and leave it at that! Even if we were to reduce all this to Dalmatia, do you know any more about where Saint Jerome, one of the greatest doctors of the Church, was born? Ask any ten thousand people you happen to meet on the streets of New York, London, or Shanghai, or all across the vast networks of main streets throughout this land and in foreign lands, and ask these people, or any random dozen of them, where's Dalmatia? Of course, you have to know that the most you are likely to learn from almost anyone in the whole crowd is that Dalmatia's a place where large white dogs with black spots come from. And yet this is what all the reference books leave you with. They not only leave you with a good dose of incipient irascibility, mind you, but also with two successive sentences ending in prepositions!

But, dammit, they don't tell you where Dalmatia is. I found out on my own that Dalmatia is a section of Yugoslavia on the coast of the Adriatic Sea. Now is that too difficult a bit of information for the compilers of reference works to provide their readers? If you think that all this is beside the point and has nothing to do with your knowing anything about Jerome, then it is evident you don't want to know anything essentially important about him—and, what may be just about as bad as that, you don't want to know anything about people who, especially in the second half of life, share his talent for a happy and redeeming sense of irascibility. Before settling on my own re-Englishing of Plato's epigraph that heads this chapter, I had

49

thought to use our own Washington Irving's remark, "A tart temper never mellows with age, and a sharp tongue is the only edged tool that grows keener with constant use" (*The Sketch Book of Geoffrey Crayon*, 1819-20). What actually occurs, I think Irving wanted to say, is that the tart temper of age becomes more pointed and pertinent, more filled with the explosive energies of acquired wisdom, than ever was possible in either one's earlier or even middle years. Irascibility in the young is intolerable. It is intolerable, of course, because the young do not yet possess the acquired wisdom that comes from, if nothing else, the whole life experience itself. Irascibility in the young is merely bad manners, while, in the old, a genuine gift for the joys of irascibility is all too frequently taken to be an ill and complaining disposition. Nonsense, I say, for we simply know that it's dumb and stupid for the clerks of information not to tell us where Dalmatia is, and the difference is that we don't hesitate to say so.

Jerome is our patron saint. He has to be my premium saint for the elderly, because he represents to me one who eternally opposed the cant and hypocrisy of the age. There is no job more important to the writer—or, for that matter, more important to one's state of mental health and general equilibrium—than standing in eternal opposition to the cant and hypocrisy of the age. Let me tell you how this can be done from two extremely divergent points of view. I mean, more precisely, how this is done in two distinctly different writers: John Henry Newman (1801-1890) and H. L. Mencken (1880-1956). What they had in common, of course, was a consummate sense of prose style. I have also to tell you at this point that I derive an almost visceral and sensuous enjoyment from reading the English prose styles of writers who were absolute masters of their craft.

I would add to Newman and Mencken the name of George Bernard Shaw, who wrote some four volumes of music criticism before he became the great playwright and dramatist known to the world today. I continue to read all their prose for pure enjoyment, but the marvelously added dimension is that each of them, in his own way, was a first-rate enemy of the cant and hypocrisy of their own age: Newman in a very noble and yet sensitively and classical way; Mencken in the formation of an American prose style more set to its purpose than any other produced in our time; and Shaw for simply being delightfully irascible and, except for an occasional gaff, a nevertheless perceptive critic of that art toward which all others tend for their own perfection.

I therefore value Jerome as an original in whom are still embodied all the best qualities of learning, scholarship and perception of the age—though, for myself, one must add, I know not a thing about Greek or Latin studies. I do know, however, that Jerome was one of the great doctors of the Church and arguably the most learned of the Latin Fathers. All who love Holy Scripture must remain, as they say, forever in his debt. But I love him for other very human and even endearing traits as well. For instance, he wrote many letters and some of the best of them were addressed to Saint Augustine of Hippo. He had, when he wanted to use it, a nicely ironic tone of voice that had the effect of impaling a butterfly on a velvet cushion—and, intellectually speaking, of course, Augustine was no butterfly. Here is part of Letter No. 68 in John J. O'Meara's excellent *An Augustine Reader* (Image Books. Doubleday, New York, 1973):

51

> *"Far be it from me to presume to attack anything which your grace has written. For it is enough for me to prove my own views without controverting what others hold. But it is well-known to one of your wisdom that everyone is satisfied with his own opinion, and that it is puerile self-sufficiency to seek, as young men have of old been accustomed to do, to gain glory to one's own name by assailing men who have become renowned. I am not so foolish as to think myself insulted by the fact that you give an explanation different from mine; since you, on the other hand, are not wronged by my views being contrary to those which you maintain. But that is the kind of reproof by which friends may truly benefit each other, when each, not seeing his own bag of faults, observes, as Persius has it, the wallet borne by the other. Let us say further, love one who loves you, and do not because you are young challenge a veteran in the field of Scripture. I have had my time, and have run my course to the utmost of my strength. It is but fair that I should rest. . . ."*

Those last few sentences and also following the ellipsis, which of course you should look up for yourself, still retain an undeniable freshness in what seems to me one of the finest brief descriptions of retirement you are likely to find anywhere today. It puts the upstart Augustine in his place, at least temporarily, and warns us all that the wisdom of experience is a form of knowledge which we dismiss at our own risk. Indeed, longevity itself is a waste of time unless accompanied by an increase in wisdom. It is a lesson which the young are hard put to learn on their own, and which in fact they seldom appreciate, and in the nature of things probably cannot. I think that wisdom is largely a matter of perspective, from a vantage point in the second half of life, that is simply not available to us in the first half of life. When I was young in years and sweet in the tooth, to say nothing of soft in the head, my point of perspective was invariably aimed from low to high. I not only looked up to my betters, such as they were, but even deferred to the most ordinary thoughts and opinions of my peers. It never occurred to me that my opinions might be just as good as theirs. I looked up to college students as beings from a state of life hardly to be attained, while priests and seminarians were utterly beyond the pale.

In the perspective of the second half of life, however, I have experienced a glorious change of view. Instead of looking up, I find myself looking benignly down and especially through. I don't look down in any contemptuous sense, but from a point of view which, I am now sure, affords one a greater sense and appreciation of the reality of things. I look and listen to college kids who seem to me like mumbling organisms of rank inarticulation, and the sermons of priests are so filled with banality and ineptitude, both in concept and expression, while lacking at the same time the slightest spark of spiritual inspiration, that you wonder how the Good News has come to be perpetuated in any sense at all. What the world generally holds up to itself as examples of self-fulfilling achievements, I take to be crushing mediocrities not to be endured. Television, of course, is the most crushing mediocrity of them all; and the cruel and utterly mindless music of our time is an assault upon the gift of hearing. You cannot read the newspaper or the various periodicals without confirming them as annals of the prevailing idiocies of our time. In the Church, I am sure that the neo-Gnosticism of our media-conscious priests and nuns would be incisively scored by Saint Jerome himself. It was not in his nature to avoid a good and worthwhile fight.

It is ironical that Jerome often got into trouble under the most innocent of circumstances. In Rome, while in the service of his protector and patron, Pope Damasus, Jerome formed what was probably the first ladies' sodality in western Christendom. (Since that kind of association may still be lodged in the memories of people who are most likely to read this book, I shall not bother to explain to all the postconciliar kiddies exactly what a ladies' sodality was before we suddenly became the autonomous People of God and started telling off those by now outdated pastors how to run their parishes). In any case, it was Jerome, who, in the waning of the fourth century, organized some Roman ladies of the highest rank in order to study Holy Scripture and perhaps thus to be drawn into a more ascetic and prayerful mode of life than Roman society was accustomed to in those days. Roman society, moreover, was singularly devoted to its skills and accomplishments in the various arts of human depravity and therefore took extreme exception to Jerome's reforming interference. Jerome initiated a series of sermons against the pagan life of the city and even dared to criticize the flagrant behavior of the most powerful and influential Romans, but he went altogether too far when he started to admonish the women of Rome on the virtues of a chaste and even celibate life. This, of course, struck at the very heart of Roman commerce in its chief trade and preoccupation—*la dolce vita* and all its most profitable effects.

When Pope Damasus died in 384, Jerome and many of his followers all but fled to the East, or at least they had the good sense to know that they were no longer wanted in Rome. But is it fair to say that it was

Jerome's irascible nature which had caused him to make such important enemies in Rome? One can readily see how the Dominican reformer Savonarola, many centuries later, might have upset a few people here and there with the severity and rigor of his reforms, but Jerome was not his prototype in these matters. I think it was Jerome's intelligence and learning that got him into trouble with the authorities. If there is anything that a politician fears, however arrogant and pretentious he may be, it is confrontation with a type of critical intelligence which is far more effective than his own—and, worse, which is in fact directed against him. This is why, in 386, Jerome was forced to settle in Bethlehem, there to be joined by Saint Paula and others in a community of religious life which offered hospitality to travelers and free schooling in Latin and Greek for the children of the area. In Rome, the enemies of Jerome had already seen to the making of rumors that would call into question his relationship with Paula, the wealthy widow of a Roman senator, who, in Bethlehem, would now establish three convents for women and a monastery for men, with the entire community under the general direction of Saint Jerome. Paula learned Latin, Greek and Hebrew, and probably assumed a personal relationship to Jerome not unlike that of, say, Mrs. Kathleen Morrison to the late poet Robert Frost. Paula was in herself a remarkable woman, and the daughter she had taken with her to Bethlehem would also become Saint Eustochium. So much, then, for all those Roman rumors.

The point is that as a role-model for people in the world, who, though consciously and even serenely situated in the second half of life, still happen to live in the real world itself, Jerome presents for our benefit not only a lofty (and often too rigorous) religious ideal but he also provides a practical means to resist the innumerable follies of our time. It is not required of us that we should quietly tolerate the massive incompetence of the postal delivery system, for example, or to suffer in silence the fact that most of our manufactured gimmickeries and major appliances do not last much beyond the point of their last payments. Jerome once wrote a letter to Augustine that took some nine years to fall into the hands of the recipient, without either one of them missing a beat of the argument, but that is no reason why elderly folk should now be inundated with junk mail that is sourced in the unscrupulous methods of entrepreneurs who have somehow gotten your name off the latest Social Security retirement listings. Jerome and his famed irascibility today would make instant enemies of those who run bad nursing homes and of other experts who have organized hospitals with little or no regard for the elderly or dying patient. Politically, with any given election safely out of the way, there is always the usable threat to cut the earned benefits of the elderly retired. This country does not respect the idea of vulnerability, and therefore has done little to protect either end of the life spectrum—from unborn children at one end to the very old at the other.

I think that we are justified in invoking Jerome against these vast and indifferent follies. I like to entertain the notion that we would have attacked our secular excesses as vigorously and as thoroughly as he demolished some of the leading errors of his own time. He defended celibacy when it was clearly unpopular to do so, as it is again today, especially among the neo-Gnostic elitists, when hardly a priest remains alive and functioning who has not suffered an all but wholly disabling "identity crisis." They naïvely presume that marriage, for instance, could very well solve all their problems, whereas such a sense of unreality is all the more likely to increase them and lead to even greater crises. Jerome was one of the first to see through Pelagianism, a heresy derived from a benighted Irish monk named Pelagius (355-425), who, come to think of it, may actually have been a perfectly normal Englishman. Jerome also knew enough about biblical exegesis to put Origen (185-254) in his place. Meanwhile, through all this, Jerome was steadily proceeding with the crowning work of his life—the translation of the Bible from Hebrew and Greek into the Latin, which, since the thirteenth century, has been known as "the Vulgate." This version remained the official text of the Bible for the Catholic Church until 1979, some fifteen hundred and fourteen years later, when Pope John Paul II replaced it with the New Vulgate. Jerome's achievement remains a prodigious monument of scholarship to which practically all English translations today owe some tribute and gratitude. Perhaps the finest one-volume biblical commentary produced by contemparory Catholic scholarship is named after him, *The Jerome Biblical Commentary* (1968), with the formidable El Greco portrait of the saint on the front of the dust jacket.

It is ironic, in the end, that one of Jerome's greatest controversies, his denunciation of Pelagianism, was at least partly responsible for his undoing. Of course, I mean by his undoing that the small Mediterranean world itself seemed all at once to become unraveled. With the great scriptural works of Jerome nearly completed and with the commentaries and letters accumulating in various hands and places, like a fruitful harvest, the task was finished just about four years into the fifth century. Soon after 404, however, reverberations from the sack of Rome by the tyrant Alaric reached all the way to Bethlehem with the arrival of refugees and other, as we now say, displaced persons. Raids by the Huns and Isaurians extended into Bethlehem itself. But the sense of irony mentioned only a moment ago had to do with the ensuing attacks by a group of armed Pelagian monks, no less, on Jerome's religious houses in the town where Jesus himself was born. Jerome managed to escape unharmed, but the monasteries were burned, gutted and left utterly demolished and poverty-stricken. It is no wonder Jerome lapsed into a long illness and died at last, in 420, some four years after these tragic occurrences. Though played out at the end, Jerome was a man of such tremendous energies that we still feel the effects of his extraordinary genius and spiritual influence today.

It may be thought necessary by scholars and churchmen of our own time to somehow resolve the matter of Jerome's intemperateness in controversy with other scholars, with even a few best friends, and personages of rank. He would have embarrassed the ecumenical movement among the Christian churches and non-Christian religions that many observers now rank as one of the most notable achievements of the postconciliar age. His opponents often suffered the untoward effects of his monumental impatience, but this was probably due as much to the power and thrust of his intellect as it was to the alleged virulence of a flawed personality. He could not see why others failed at once to perceive what was already perfectly clear to him. The theory has been suggested that the classical formalities of rhetorical dispute in those days, when the struggle for ideas seemed nothing less than a struggle for power and survival, had an effect on Jerome which at length caused him to erupt in especially insulting attacks against his unfortunate opponents. I think it is more realistic to recognize the fact that Jerome's personality, which was also known to be idealistic and kindly toward those less fortunate and gifted than himself, was certainly formed long before he had learned the models for classical disputation. Jerome was Jerome, and there's no sense at this late date in trying to make him a saint in the way we think saints ought to be for the sake and purpose of our own edification. He had no time for the indulgences of these ordinary pieties, which, to the rest of us, may seem profound and everlasting verities.

Taken all in all—that is to say, taking Jerome as he actually was—what more could we want from a saint for those not only in the onset of their maturity but even more for those already involved in the saint-making of one's own character and destiny? If we do not take Jerome at his best, we shall sooner or later get him at his worst. I'll take him both at his best and worst, because his worst was nothing more than short-fused manners when dealing with oafs, pretentious simpletons and ignoramuses at the academic level. For them he kept the swords of his invective all the more sharply honed. I know I shouldn't, but I want you in turn to know that I unabashedly love it. I shall roll unashamed in the sins of Jerome! I shall indulge the pleasures of pure irascibility! (This is not for the young, mind you, but only for those who have fairly well paid their dues in full.) I shall no longer tremble in remorse when I have walked mentally away from someone who, in conversation with me, takes more than twenty seconds to complete a thought or a sentence in response to something I have said. We have at last found the saint who has solved the problem—or who has at least mitigated the human dilemma—of a kind of holiness so inhibiting that it would certainly damage, if not destroy, that very wholeness of the person we must present to the Creator at last, for whatever we may be worth, in all our pristine identity and human uniqueness.

References and Suggested Readings

1. *An Augustine Reader*, edited by John J. O'Meara. Image Books, Doubleday, New York, 1973.
2. *The Jerome Biblical Commentary*, edited by Raymond E. Brown, S.S., Joseph A. Fitzmyer, S.J., and Roland E. Murphy, O.Carm. Prentice-Hall, Englewood Cliffs, N.J., 1968.

5

Saint Francis of Assisi

Reconciliation With Nature

Nature has some perfections, to show that she is the image of God; and some defects, to show that she is only His image.
—Blaise Pascal, *Pensées*

Francis of Assisi (Francesco Bernardine) was born about 1181, the son of a wealthy silk merchant. As a youth, he led a somewhat frivolous and carefree life. Thinking that warfare itself was a lark, Francis found himself involved in matters of civil strife. He was taken prisoner in 1202, then released, sought worldly pleasures again and eventually suffered a serious illness. At Spoleto, he experienced a vision of Christ that was radically to alter his whole way of life. He was now caring for the poor and the sick, living in poverty, and rebuilding churches that had fallen into disrepair. His father not only disinherited his irresponsible son but, worse, disowned him outright. Francis, at Portiuncula, now took to preaching as well and began to gather some disciples and followers, many of them leading citizens, others commonfolk and tradesmen. In 1210, Pope Innocent III granted to Francis and his followers permission to follow a rule of spiritual life that took into account the pragmatic realities as well. Two years later, with the help of Saint Clare, he founded the first community of Poor Ladies. He sustained the marks of the stigmata in 1224 and died in great suffering two years later. His feast day is October 4.

FRANCIS of Assisi is everybody's saint, young and

old, but not for always identical reasons. The reasons for his appeal to the young, I think, may be largely sentimental. That he loved birds and animals and practically everything else in sight is a fact which is likely to keep him in good standing with all creatures great and small, including, of course, children in their innocence, crones in their irascibility, and self-styled countrymen in their dotage. This is not necessarily the Saint Francis I prefer to take seriously as a role-model for the second half of life—or, as I was about to say sentimentally, for the autumn and winter seasons of our declining years. I don't take too fondly to people who talk to the birds, and also think that anyone would be ill-advised to go around patting the wild wolf on its head or trying to make deals with the species on matters of its bad behavior. Like the exciting nature writer Barry Holstun Lopez, I have inordinate admiration for the legend of Francis and the wolf of Gubbio; but it really wasn't necessary to have made a moral fable of a rare but natural act of human feeling extended to a wild creature that was only fulfilling its own nature—that was, in other words, simply being true to its own *wolfness*. Mr. Barry Lopez himself, in his already definitive study on the subject, *Of Wolves and Men* (1978), grants to Francis an unusual, if not unique, sense of compassion for all creatures and component parts of the natural order, including the shaggy ravager of Gubbio, and which sense of compassion, by the way, was all but unknown to either the Church or to society at large in the thirteenth century. This may have been the true miracle of Gubbio.

So this, too, begins to indicate something of the approach to Francis of Assisi (otherwise laminated over the centuries with merely pious sentiments) that now seems the only tolerable approach to one of the authentically burnt men of Christ. I want to look at him as a man who, perhaps more than any other, has reconciled our human nature with that great chain of being to which we are necessarily linked in our earthly existence on this blue and green and cloud-capped planet. It is also true that each of us is going back into the earth again, one way or another, to be hurled round and round, as the poet Wordsworth said, with rocks and stones and trees and even, I might add, with all the stars and planets themselves whirling about in a universe which is still a glorious and impenetrable mystery to us. Our earth may be only a tent pitched against the encroachment of the universal dark, but it is all we have of human habitation until that time when our spirit shall find its ultimate solace and security in the very heart and nest of God. I think the life of Francis tells us this.

I once wrote an early essay, "Pian d'Arca and Walden Pond," that was printed more than twenty-five years ago in a small Franciscan magazine called *The Cord*, published by St. Bonaventure College, at Olean, in upper New York state, where Thomas Merton once taught English shortly after his conversion to the Church. As the title of that essay indicates, it is a comparison of the attitudes toward nature that are held by Francis of Assisi, on the one hand, and Henry Thoreau of Concord, on the other. I live less than a half hour's drive from Concord and often visit there in order to take in something of the original ambience of that remarkable community and countryside which managed to produce so many luminaries in our literature and history. Nevertheless, that long ago, I also intuited the shattering difference which still separates an essentially New England sense of aloofness (Transcendentialism) plus a romantic worship of nature (Pantheism) from the warmth, immediacy, and sacramental presence in Mediterranean (Catholic) spirituality. Thoreau knew everything in nature except its sacramental presence. He probably would have enjoyed the kinetic energy of Gerard Manley Hopkins' poetry, but he wouldn't have known why it is there. I was beginning to find that in the company of my two friends, Francis and Henry, it was I who remained most ill at ease.

Updated, and in the sense that these essays in the art of Christian aging are written, I have to tell you why Henry does not wear too well for those in the second half of life. To begin with, he had a curiously flawed attitude toward the elderly. Indeed, I find it incredible that in all the critical attention that has been given to Thoreau and his masterpiece, *Walden* (1854), so few commentators have cited his contempt for the elderly. In the celebrated opening essay, "Economy," Thoreau is as juvenile toward the elderly as he is sophomoric toward the complexities of the economic order itself, even in his own time, for anyone other than a fairly well-off bachelor. There are other denigrations of the elderly scattered throughout the *Journal* (1837-1861). When he was thirty-four, Thoreau had already concluded that after some three decades on the planet he had not heard so much as a syllable of usable advice from his seniors. They could tell him nothing, he said, because they knew nothing to the purpose. About a year later, he took pains to muse upon the elderly again and decided that they were as "mouldy as the grave" and reminded him of "earthworms and mole crickets." At thirty-nine, he noted in his *Journal* the obstinacy of old age, but without wondering any further why this might be so, and certainly without determining whether obstinacy in old age might not be a defensible tactic for survival. At forty, he partly redeemed himself, again in the *Journal*, with the incomparable passage about meeting Brooks Clark, "eighty and bent like a bow," hastening along the old Carlisle road in mid-autumn. But Thoreau's attitude toward the elderly, I'm afraid, had already been well established as something other than redolent with Franciscan charity toward all God's creatures—even to pitiable human beings, perhaps, as distinguished from his "little fishy friend" in the pond.

The only scholar I know who has called into question the matter of Thoreau's attitudes toward aging and death itself is Harvard professor of English and American literature, Joel Porte. I persist in examining the question, moreover, because these were not fugitive speculations on Thoreau's part; but they were, as he would himself say, part and parcel of his vision of life. It is of particular relevance, I think, that Thoreau is so frequently taken to be the secular replacement in the New World for the essentially sacramental love of man and nature that is exemplified in the life and passion of Francis of Assisi. Thoreau's first of only two published works in his lifetime, *A week on the Concord and Merrimack Rivers* (1849), plus, of course, *Walden*, are secularist liturgies for a cult of youth dedicated to an order of nature in which one is eternally disappointed to find gall in the shrub oak and insects infesting the lily pads. Thoreau had all but developed a phobia of some kind or other when, in walking through Concord's gentle woods, he encountered the malevolent fungus. Fungus became his central image for the process of decay and dying. The pyramids of Egypt, he said, were vast toadstools; a priest "the fungus of the graveyard" and "mildew of the tomb." I conclude these brief evidences of the

65

Thoreau we do not often meet, especially in the edifying commentaries of his enthusiasts, with a sentence on Thoreau's theory of art from Joel Porte's invaluable study, *Emerson and Thoreau* (Wesleyan University Press, Middletown, Conn., 1966): "Thoreau's theory of art," Professor Porte wrote, "is a theory built on the illusory hope of perennial youth and in frantic defiance of the exigencies of age." So much then, for Thoreau and the elderly.

This is why I say that, as far as our reconciliation with nature is concerned, our patron saint has to be Francis and, God knows, not Thoreau. Our coming of age and our hastening slowly to reconciliation with nature, toward origins sourced in the very Godhead itself, are measures we should not attempt to diminish with dalliances to youth or that we should unduly inhibit with morbid fears of death. It is soon enough when Donkey Body, as Francis called the construct of his own physical appearance, shall little by little fail to carry us to the places we want to go. He also called his body the brother of his soul, but, all the same, admonished Donkey Body to pull himself together so that he could go teach the minstrels a new song which the Father had just given him. At this point, I am reminded of what, for me, is one of the most beautiful and touching passages in the New Testament. I mean that incandescent Chapter 21 of John's Gospel, all of it, but in this case verse 18 in particular, wherein Jesus says to Simon Peter, in *The Jerusalem Bible* translation (Doubleday, New York, 1966):

> I tell you most solemnly,
> when you were young
> you put on your own belt
> and walked where you liked;
> but when you grow old

you will stretch out your hands,
and somebody else will put a belt around you
and take you where you would rather not go.

The young, being young, will never fully understand those lines; but everyone in the second half of life will not only understand but feel what they mean. Francis even then, confined to his pallet, praised Brother Sun in the morning and knew that the nighttime visitation of his Sister Death was near at hand.

It is a curious coincidence that Francis of Assisi and Henry Thoreau of Concord died at the same age, forty-five, having lived close to nature, though each in his own and vastly different way. As often occurs in stories having to do with the deaths of great men, the ones about Francis and Henry are so keeping with their separate characters that one may count them as certainly more factual than legendary. Thoreau on his deathbed was asked whether he had made his peace with God, and he replied matter-of-factly that he had never quarreled with Him. If that is so, as all accounts testify, it was only because Thoreau had hardly ever talked to Him in the first place. The point is that Thoreau's reply was thoroughly Thoreauvian, a wry joke and ironic pun at the end. If Thoreau's very proper Concord neighbors were demurely scandalized by this sort of response, so had the haughty and practical Brother Elias long ago taken keen exception to Francis singing the "Praises to All Creatures" as he lay so near to death. Elias was the leader of the Franciscan order at that time, but Francis was still its heart and soul as well as its voice and song.

At the end, Francis asked his disciples to turn him around, facing Assisi, so that he could see the town one last time and bless it. Concord is known as a place filled with the New England worthies who were Thoreau's contemporaries, while Assisi is known for the presence and spirit of Francis alone. This in itself is a delicious and perhaps Chestertonian paradox, for I like to think that the great English essayist, who loved Francis dearly, might have added on his own that, though Thoreau and Francis happened to die at the same age, the one died eternally old and the other eternally young. It was a question, I think, of a certain disposition of the soul.

It is also a question that has to do with how each of them was reconciled to nature. I believe that Thoreau was reconciled to nature as a form of pantheism and that Francis was reconciled to nature as a form of both immanence and transcendence. Pantheism (or nature itself identified as God) is the chief doctrine in the secularist religion of American Romanticism founded by Thoreau's mentor and neighbor, Ralph Waldo Emerson, and which the so-called Sage of Concord early recognized in the new barbaric yawp of the poet Walt Whitman, and so on down to some of the major poets of our time—T.S. Eliot excepted—and culminating, logically enough, in the solipsism of Wallace Stevens. I don't want the going to get sticky at this point, however, but simply suggest that in the second half of life we ought to have become poets of the ultimate realities and not poets of the imagination only. Also, I here use the term poets as the more fully realized human beings we should strive to become as we round out the number of our days on the planet. It is primarily in this sense that Francis was one of the greatest poets who ever lived and only secondarily in the sense that he had also composed some of the most luminous hymns to creation ever written by men or angels. Thoreau wrote essays of consummate prose and learning, but the simple letters, prayers and poems of Francis are like a Fifth Gospel to the New Testament.

The essential difference between Francis and Thoreau cannot be either overlooked or casually ignored. If it is, the tendency will be toward a sentimentalization of Thoreau, not Francis, as in the case of the American naturalist Joseph Wood Krutch who saw little to be gained from Saint Francis preaching to the birds, when what we should have hoped for is that the birds might have preached to us moderns.

This, of course, is sentimental nonsense and probably misses the point that the only way the birds can preach to us, marked as we are with the awesome gift of free will, lies in our abiding realization that the birds are already completely what God intended they should be. The fact is, too, that we are faced with yet another paradox: for while Francis intuitively recognized God's creatures as lower in the hierarchy of life forms, he treated them almost as equals; whereas the modern "nature lover," while claiming the equalization of man and creatures, treats them as inferiors.

There is something condescending, perhaps even maudlin, about Thoreau's having had "a little fishy friend" in the pond, though the Concord ladies at their teas no doubt loved the idea. But there is genuine love in the salutations of Francis to Sister Swallow, Sister Cicada, Brother Hare, Brother Fish, etc. Even the great inanimates received his all-inclusive love: Brother Sun, Sister Moon, Brother Wind, Sister Water; and it was an individualized love, not an abstraction of everything all rolled into one and labeled Nature, with a capital N, for indisputable significance. Francis was the world's best answer to pantheism, I think, because he rejected utterly the notion there is nothing left that shoots the spirit on toward still greater glory.

There is nothing like love to shoot the spirit on, and this is why Francis makes all the difference to us. He went beyond romantic love, which existed briefly in the province of our youth, to that order of love which can be acquired only through the pains and anguishes of the life experience itself. This is why it is so important to keep love alive and growing the older we ourselves grow. Have you ever noticed the devastating but lovely candor of people who have grown beautifully older? When we are older we should not have to put up with forced conditions of boredom and unthinking stupidity on the part of those who should know better than to do half the things they do—or, inversely, don't do. I have of late walked out on sermons so dumb and droningly irrelevant that I could no longer bear to wait them out. If Francis had been as dismal as the preachers and preaching deacons of our day, taken all in all, there would certainly have been no Franciscan movement to refresh and revivify the world. I do not have to tell the beautifully old about a new law that is automatically built into one's advancing perspectives: Do not suffer fools gladly. In that admonition, however, let the adverb stand as a word to the wise.

The wisdom of Francis abides. He not only continues to reconcile us to nature, in our own time, but he would also alter a view of the world which was gaining prominence simultaneously with his own appearance on the scene as a new and startling imitation of Christ. What was that world view? In the twelfth century, the Benedictine abbess of a convent on the Rhine, Saint Hildegard, experienced a series of apocalyptic visions. For nearly a decade, the "Sibyl of the Rhine," as she was called, dictated accounts of these visions to her secretary. The writings became known to high churchmen and scholars for the awesome picture they presented of a world about to suffer the most terrible and terrifying events. The Cistercian monk Joachim of Flora, also in the twelfth century and a fragment of the thirteenth, had even greater visions that were nothing less than cosmic in proportion. He projected an elaborate Trinitarian vision to account for all creation itself and for the history of the world, with the Age of the Holy Spirit about to appear, and monks especially in a favored position to receive it. (Incidentally, in an interview with Thomas Merton, I once extrapolated something like this Trinitarian vision of the cosmos without my ever having heard of one Joachim of Flora whose teachings, I was both bemused and dismayed to learn, had been advanced by some Franciscan extremists and later condemned by the Lateran Council in 1215). In any case, such was the intellectual and spiritual disposition of Western Christendom when Francis of Assisi came to set it right—which is to say, in harmony with God and nature again.

The world was never the same after Francis had lived in it, and you cannot say that of many men and women, or even of many certified saints. In him were the beginnings of a new and vigorous poetry. His sermon to the birds, at Pian d'Arca, literally breathed new life into painting, giving it form and color and movement, for it was that same sermon to the birds which opened the eyes of medieval man to the natural world around him in a way that he had not heretofore perceived. So one is not surprised to learn that Roger Bacon, who is called the father of modern science, was not only a medieval man but a Franciscan scholar as well. Science, when true to its discipline, may therefore trace its origin to the Christian concept of nature. Such a statement may provoke a rollicking outburst in the closed ranks of scientism; but, whether we like it

71

or not, the choice is of the either/or sort: Either we grope around in protoplasm and blind chance or we look toward God and divine grace.

The choice, after all, is Franciscan in its simplicity. It was for Francis, indeed, not so much a matter of choice as the inevitability of something already known. The ultimate reality to which we are the witnesses is no less than Jesus Christ as the center and circumference of all we know or can possibly know in the end. It is not even empathy that matters, but redeeming love; not protoplasm, but the salvific blood of Christ; not the cosmic and indifferent All, but God as He is in Himself. All this, if not stated in literal and exact terms, is nevertheless implicit in the life of Francis of Assisi. He celebrated it in the sermon to the birds and he sang about it in the Canticle of the Sun. His theology could not help but break into song even unto death. Francis was the kind of troubador who would put the world in tune; and this is exactly what he did, for he restored to nature and to our human nature something of the innocence that once was known in Paradise—and lost there, until supernatural grace alone shall stay us from confusion once again and assure us of that blessed heaven we still yearn for. Above all, I think, Francis of Assisi possessed a sense of the divine folly—or, perhaps more accurately, it possessed him—and which happens also to be a necessary attribute of the soul in the second half of life. We must be ready to travel lightly, without encumbering possessions, and always at a moment's notice.

References and Suggested Readings

1. *Emerson and Thoreau*, by Joel Porte. Wesleyan University Press, Middletown, Conn., 1966.

2. *The Seven Miracles of Gubbio and the Eighth*: A Parable, Raymond Leopold Bruckberger, O.P. McGraw-Hill, New York, 1948.

3. *Brother Francis*: An Anthology of Writings by and About St. Francis of Assisi, edited by Lawrence Cunningham. Harper and Row, New York, 1972.

4. *Francis of Assisi*: The Wandering Years, by Anthony Mockler. Phaidon / E. P. Dutton. Oxford and New York, 1976.

5. *St. Francis of Assisi*, by G. K. Chesterton. Image Books. Doubleday, New York, 1957.

Job

The Problem of Suffering

We must die young or suffer much.

—Portuguese proverb

Job, the main character in one of the indisputable literary masterpieces of the Bible, is immediately identified as a man in the land of Uz, probably south of Edom, a territory that extended south of the Dead Sea to the Gulf of Aqaba. It is all but certain that he was a well-known, if not indeed famous, figure in patriarchal history. There is a reference to Job in Ezekiel 14:14, 20. It is generally agreed that the author of the Book of Job was an Israelite and that in all probability Job himself was an Edomite. We know that he was a man of property and extremely wealthy. From the prologue to the Book of Job, we know the extent of his family, the sizes of his herds of sheep and oxen, and we soon become more than casually acquainted with Job's friends — particularly Eliphaz, Bildad, and Zophar—possibly the three most contentious friends in the annals of recorded history. Epitomizing the problem of human suffering, the figure of Job has inspired Western culture with some of its greatest expressions in art, depth-psychology, moral theology, and philosophical speculation in general.

"SAINT Job?" she asked. "Since when?"

"Since about the beginning of the fifth century B.C., most scholars say, or even as early as the third, when the story of Job became a matter of the public

74

record and which has thus come down to us — extraordinary, just to think of it—to this very day."

"Yes, if you say so, but still why *Saint* Job? I'd always thought that saints had to originate from the Christian or post-Christian era, so to speak, and also had to be declared saints through an elaborate process of canonization."

"First, I use the term both lightly and seriously at the same time, considering anyone a saint, known or unknown, who has been touched in a very special way by supernatural grace—and, God knows, literally speaking, Job was so touched by God. Some might say that he was more than touched, he was clobbered."

"Crude," she said, "but to the point."

"Secondly," I added, "I have to make Job a saint in order to include him in the book of saints for the elderly I'm doing. Can you think of a better reason?"

I was talking with Elizabeth, my wife, who loves especially her daughter, other people in general, children in particular, saints for special causes, stars of a summer night, flowers and fruit trees in spring, grazing cows (because of their large and limpid eyes), the New England woodlands in autumn, creweling in winter, the Clydesdale horses, and me, in approximately that order.

For these and other reasons, I love Elizabeth inordinately, which is really the best and only way to love anyone at all. It is a kind of love which the young, in their halcyon years, do not yet realize shall one day be either increased or sadly diminished by the pain and suffering of great personal ordeals. For us, and especially for Elizabeth, these ordeals have existed in complex forms of physical suffering caused by illnesses. In our younger days, chronologically speaking, I used to call her Betty most of the time. But when I had later seen her suffering so much and summoning her great resources of courage and determination to be back again at the heart and center of her home and family, I looked more deeply into her eyes than I had ever seen before, and for some reason I called her Elizabeth and still do, almost regularly now, for I knew that we had reached a new plateau in our life together. We had already been through many hardships, especially during the trying days of separation during World War II, which nobody in our family circle has really known anything about; but now suffering and pain have become part and parcel of our shared daily existence. Even so, more than ever, Elizabeth remains the spirit and substance of our home and life together.

For people in the second half of life, indeed, suffering and the onset of suffering become something quite other than abstract problems in moral theology. Avoid the definition of suffering by any philosopher who has not suffered. It is enough that we accept here the figure of Job as that of a man who suffered. I have listened to a cassette tape recording of a learned biblical theologian, whose name would be immediately recognizable as perhaps the outstanding Catholic scholar in his field, talking about the problem of Job and human suffering; and yet, in my lowly and amateurish view, it is a discourse that has come to naught. It largely misses the point that pain is not necessarily a synonym for suffering and that the problem of evil, in like manner, is not necessarily the major concern of the Book of Job in the first place. Suffering itself is not wholly what the Book of Job is about, at least not in strictly human terms, for in human terms alone, of course, suffering must always remain an inexplicable curse. It seems to me self-evident that this great book of the Bible has to do chiefly with Job's essential fidelity to

God despite all the incredible assaults which God Himself permits the Adversary to launch against the hapless man of Uz.

It has bothered us no end—and perhaps to no end as well—that God should have allowed such a game to be played against His servant Job. If you settle for playing a game in which anything goes, short of death, then it is almost certain that the subject of the game will end up enjoying nothing whatever, short of life itself. To lift us out of this state of absurdity, we have only to realize Job as a prefiguration of the suffering Christ, and even of His resurrection, through fidelity as both a kind of heroic virtue and reconversion to the God of all creation. Otherwise, the contest for the soul of Job becomes unrealistic and absurd unless there is something extraordinarily significant at stake. What's at stake with Job, indeed, is nothing other than the integrity granted to us in the gift of our human free will—that very gift, perhaps, which we stole from Paradise.

Meanwhile, back on earth, suffering remains. The trouble is that we have tried to do away with the bane of human suffering in the world as if it were a bad decision handed down by the U.S. Supreme Court. We consider it unclinical and unsanitary to have to bear any semblance of suffering, and it has become both the art and science of the mortician to protect us, at exorbitant costs, from this last of the world's great realities. It is not so much suffering as the idea of death that we cannot abide. Evelyn Waugh's incisive little classic, *The Loved One* (1948), is a devastating indictment of the American way of death, though not quite devastating enough, apparently, for we still insist that our coffins should be covered with luridly green artificial grass and that we should turn discreetly away from the gaping hole of our last earthly home in order not to hear the raw clods of earth falling with dull thuds on the roofs of our unrest. I say our unrest, of course, because it is we the living who turn and walk quietly away from this witness to our one and only earthbound future. I want to know why we take such exception to the inevitability of human suffering, when He who was faultless Himself, our Lord and Savior Jesus Christ, chose to suffer so that we might at last know a time when no more tears shall fall.

I do not say these things for the morose pleasure of it, but only because I know that men and women in their late sixties and early seventies cease to find it shocking to speak of such matters. As that arguably finest English essayist, William Hazlitt, once said: "No young man believes he shall ever die." The eldering toward God, however, know they shall die in due season; and like the road duly taken instead of idly not taken, that makes all the difference. And yet, I fear, the knowledge that there are two diverging roads there at all, one which goes to the far mountains and the other through fields of fresh daisies, seems no guarantee that one way lies wisdom and the other a labyrinth of follies. I only mean to suggest that we ought not to confuse our own little problems of discomfort with the infinitely larger and profounder problem of human suffering. To many of us, I suppose, a hangnail is more intolerable than the Holocaust. The trouble is that we are beginning to treat the problem of human suffering as something to be gotten rid of and put out of sight once and for all. I have seen in suburban Catholic churches, and in my own parish church, the elimination of a central and prominently displayed crucifix as an integral part of the liturgical design and architecture of the church itself. There is no symbol of Christ

78

crucified in the design of my parish church, nor any depiction of this central act of His life in any one of the personally subscribed stained glass windows of the church, though gloriously over the altar itself there indeed looms the figure of the risen Christ. In short, we have taken Good Friday out of the parish church.

Can you believe this? We are eliminating the sign of the suffering Christ from the liturgical life of our parish churches. In an age which produced the Holocaust, I find this reprehensible. It is my opinion that every Christian church, and especially every Roman Catholic church, should continue to offer as the central feature of its liturgical design the figure of the suffering and crucified Christ. Moreover, I dare to think of the suffering of the Jews as also daily recalled and witnessed in this prophetic way. Though I do not think that the sufferings of Job were the frivolous effects of a divine contestation, they were in fact a test. We are tested daily, but we are fools to try avoiding the reality that our testing of the spirit can be accomplished without any measure of human suffering. This is the sort of folly that would have tried the patience—or, more likely at last, the impatience—of Job himself.

On behalf of those now steadily growing toward union with God—meaning, of course, the authentically mature—I wonder whether the characteristic of impatience itself must always and inevitably be counted as a failure of moral virtue. In other words, cannot impatience under certain circumstances be reckoned a virtue instead? It does the heart a rare and virtuous good to hear someone say that "discontent is not necessarily a sin but a potential means of grace and that the chief crime of modern man is not impatience but the patience with which he receives the superficial panaceas of secular humanism." This is from a perfectly marvelous small book on the subject, *The Impatience of Job* (1981), by George W. Rutler, in the paperback edition recently published by Sugden, Sherwood & Company, and already, it seems to me, one of the most refreshingly honest books of the decade. Its style is reminiscent of some of the writings of Edward Dahlberg, the late extraordinary critic of American life and culture, without his sometimes overbearing use of the conceits of learning in the form of elaborate literary allusions, etc. It is as if Father Rutler, a convert from the Episcopalian Church to Catholicism, had the sensibility of a Christianized Edward Dahlberg though with a talent for references which are perfectly suited to the purpose at hand. In any case, here is a book that reminds us of the obvious: (1) that Job is quintessentially human, the only basis on which he can in fact encounter the divine perceptions at all; and (2) that he takes God seriously, while his three friends and even his own wife do not. It is little wonder that the patience of Job was sorely tried.

At this point, it is necessary to indulge a slight but very personal confession. I mean by this that what I shall say here may be more a matter for one's confessor than for the casually listening ear or roving and inattentive eye. I have suffered most of my adult life from a precipitous lack of patience, which, on many an occasion, I have later had cause to regret. I think that this flawed trait in my nature has also been coupled with a keen sense of injustice sustained from experiences of my earliest youth. I had no talent for self-defense. But where I was once given to a posture of deference that bordered on mere obsequiousness, which both my peers and elders invariably mistook for shyness, I have in the second half of life come to feel a more powerful act of mind, more willing to discern

80

and define differences, and therefore less and less willing to settle for mediocrities and the mere toleration of error. In fact, my present problem is that I have become extraordinarily impatient with people who do not catch on quickly to what you are saying, who do not respond to the point that you think you have already made luminously clear, or who choose to remain adamantly immersed in what you take to be their own acts of intolerance against others.

I am ashamed to admit that I could hardly abide the presence of a female Religious of a minor order who totally occupied, rather than shared, the same hospital room with my wife Elizabeth in her recent and perhaps most serious illness. For years now, especially just before and after Vatican Council II, it has been one of the pet preoccupations of the Religious (non-contemplative variety) to prove to the laity and themselves that they were, you know, "just like everybody else." But where does it say that it was ever required of them that their behavior should be demonstrably *worse* than anybody else's? Most of the illusions I may have once had about some of the professionally religious in the Church have long since vanished; but I had never seen anyone so arrogantly inert, to indulge an oxymoron, as this hulk of a nun utterly consumed by the Unholy Writ of continuous television game shows in the morning and soap stories in the afternoon. In visage, she was granite-like and in demeanor the same. My only point in telling you all this—though "all this" isn't the half of it—is simply to say that seldom has my patience been so sorely tested. Talk about Job, I was Job incarnate. I was therefore infuriated and ashamed at the same time: infuriated for obvious reasons having to do with the comfort of my wife; ashamed because I was so constantly near a loss of temper and in witness to the behavior of a Catholic Christian Religious who, herself, shamed each of these eternal identities which she pretended to represent. I comforted myself to think that Jesus once showed His temper when He drove the money-changers from the temple. We presume at our own risk that the chastisements of the Lord shall never apply to us, and that all we shall ever know is the beneficence of His gratuitous mercy.

This was no doubt what Job had thought before the chastisements of Yahweh were visited upon him, and neither did he get much help from his friends. Of Job's three friends—Eliphaz, Bildad, and Zophar—it is the first, Eliphaz, who is the eldest and, as Father Rutler describes him, "seems the most erect, the most proud, the most gracious, the most distinguished, the most grand, the most ornate, but unfortunately the most pompous as well." I'm afraid that as we grow older there is likely to be more of Eliphaz in us than Job, certainly a distinct preference for most of us, who would not want to invite the troubles of Job under any circumstances. It was of course Eliphaz who would suggest to Job that his troubles were of his own making, a most likely suggestion from anyone unblessed by the knowledge of suffering. In the end, all that Eliphaz could offer Job was a set of platitudes. It was these platitudes, Father Rutler says, that rendered Job almost cosmically impatient; and then adds the exquisitely perceptive observation that out of Job's resistance to the platitudes of Eliphaz and the other friends there developed the authentic personality of the man, Job, as a kind of prefiguration of that order of human realization that Jesus was to find in the plain and rugged fishermen of Galilee.

In growing older, it ought to be part of our aim to

become more like Job than like the friends who were no longer equipped to advise him and whom he would have to leave behind, unacquainted as they were with the luminous and awful knowledge that human suffering had already imparted to Job himself. Then along comes the teenager Elihu, leaping suddenly into the air (I am young, he presumes to tell Job, and you are old), who has the bright idea that pain purges us sufficiently to stand in the pure presence of God, etc., and that Job should therefore welcome this purgation by pain as a natural good. The precocious Elihu simply doesn't know what he is talking about, does not know or even allow that there might be some difference between suffering and pain, as such, and whom Job would have to leave by the side of the road in his great journey toward reconciliation with God and in defeat of the Adversary.

At last there is visited upon Job, as if to this point he hadn't had troubles enough, that devastating inquiry from the very presence of God which we must rank as probably the greatest putdown in the entire biblical literature of the Old Testament. For it is at this point, which trembles momentarily like a solitary leaf before the first onslaught of a summer storm to end all summer storms, that Job most truly confronts his Maker. As Father Rutler further suggests, it was Job who had been "demanding questions of God and trying to arraign Him"—and then what he heard indeed was that unspeakable Name saying unspeakable things: "Where were you when I laid the earth's foundations? / Tell me, since you are so well informed?" (*The Jerusalem Bible*), and so follows that incredible speech of God's, the very Yahweh at the heart of the tempest (see *Job* 38:4-11), whose name is not to be profaned by our merely human utterance. The reader is implored to go on with the test to the end of the speech, though perhaps in a translation other than that of *The Jerusalem Bible*, which, at verse 17, lapses into such a disastrous rendition as possibly to damage the whole effect.

Job is my defense and the defense of all who have nearly paid their dues in full and who still resist the unbelievable follies of those who think they know it all. They who think they know it all, however, are hardly in the position of that all-powerful God who answered Job with a divine and exalted blast of immortal poetry. We who are in our ripening majority must rejoice in this tremendous and perfectly marvelous humiliation, because, of course, what it does is to keep things in their proper perspective. From our own human perspective, however, it is not required of us that we should go on suffering fools any more gladly than we have to—and I for one do not intend to go on accommodating the cant and banality of the age for the sake of appearing to be a merely lovable progressive.

References and Suggested Readings

1. *The Impatience of Job*, by George W. Rutler, Sugden, Sherwood & Company, La Salle, Ill.,1981.
2. *Blake's Job*: William Blake's Illustrations of the Book of Job. With an Introduction and Commentary by S. Foster Damon, E.P. Dutton, New York, 1969.

7

Saint Joseph

The Anonymity of Fatherhood

When a father gives to his son, both laugh; when a son gives
to his father, both cry.

—Yiddish proverb

Joseph, husband of the Virgin Mary and foster-father of Jesus Christ, is known to us chiefly through the Gospels and particularly in the Infancy narratives related by Matthew and Luke. A builder or carpenter by trade, he was of royal lineage from the house of David and was known to be an honorable and upright man. He was no doubt a young man when betrothed to Mary, of her own age, that is, and thus all the more distressed on learning of her pregnancy, though he had not lived with her. Joseph was so distraught that only an angelic vision dissuaded him from rejecting Mary. He then took Mary as his wife and journeyed with her to Bethlehem and was with her at the birth of Jesus. He is present with Jesus and Mary in the Gospel narratives up to the time of finding the twelve-year-old Jesus discoursing with the doctors in the temple. After that event, Joseph is mentioned only once by Luke (4:22) as the father of Jesus. It is believed that he must have died before the crucifixion. Apocryphal writings are generally responsible for artistic depictions of Joseph as an old man. He has been highly favored by various popes as an exemplary model of the social message. He has feast days on March 19 and May 1.

THERE would ordinarily be no problem at all in selec-

85

ting various role-models of the father from among the great and sophisticated heroes of history, but when I came to sit down on hard rock and figure it out clearly and with all the sense of reality that I could bring to the point at hand, I had to conclude that all the truest fathers I had ever known somehow turned out to be the authentic and humble and hardworking Josephs of this world. For some years I worked in a paper mill in Boston, where my own father had himself served as its highly inventive and resourceful superintendent, and so I came to know many of the men who worked there as well. I was not treated with particular favor and had menial jobs on both the day and night shifts, which deserves mention here only because it gave me a chance to know what the editorial writers call the "workingman" on a personal and knowledgeable basis. I knew on intimate terms the lives of many hardworking Irishmen, Italians, and Poles who happened also by and large to be practicing Catholics, almost always buoyant of spirit and steady of hand, who were wholly devoted to the welfare and advancement of their families. They were the anonymous Josephs of this world.

Let me tell you that I also saw tragedy and great sorrow in the mill. The generations that I once knew there have been all but decimated by postwar changes of jobs, deaths, and retirements. The trouble is that retirement itself is taken to be a kind of death. My earliest association with the meaning of retirement had to do with a lively little chipmunk of a man, bewhiskered and beloved, who labored in his quiet and unobtrusive way for all those numberless years that were in fact duly numbered and noted by people who keep track of such things, until enough of them were accumulated for his retirement. His whole life had been fulfilled by the fact of his employment in the paper mill. Now, suddenly, he was released at the mandatory age; and one day shortly after that somebody said to me, "Did you hear about Charlie Williams (not his real name)? They found him in the river, drowned, last night. They say he just walked into the river and drowned himself." But retirement does not have to be like that dark and ominous river and Charlie Williams floating face down in its sluggish movement toward a wide and sunless sea.

It may not at first seem clear to you that these observations have anything to do with Joseph of Nazareth, but I only mean to suggest something of that level of reality at which the truly common life exists—though, by common, I do not mean ordinary or banal. The paper mill was the locus wherein many lives converged in order not only to survive but, if possible, to thrive and grow and thus witness the advance of one's sons and daughters in the then fine schools and colleges of New England. I almost daily shared lunch from a brown paper bag with the father of the seminarian who would later become Father John Joseph Wright of Boston, then Bishop of Worcester, Bishop of Pittsburgh, and then as Cardinal at the Vatican itself, Prefect of the Congregation of the Clergy throughout the Roman Catholic world. In fact, the younger Wright also worked for a time in the paper mill at Hyde Park. I still treasure an inscribed copy of the original Stratford (Boston) edition of Father John Wright's dissertation for his Doctorate in Sacred Theology, *National Patriotism in Papal Teaching* (1942), submitted to the Pontifical Gregorian University in Rome. He was then a priest of the Archdiocese of Boston and his father worked in the paper mill, a wry and sparkling little man, whose job was to weigh in bales of paper waste for recycling into bleached and reusable pulp. The elder John Wright was thus exactly what I mean by the anonymous and loving and hard-working father, the Joseph in all such men, who labors quietly and supports his family to the best of his ability. I knew another man in the paper mill who also raised a son to be an outstanding parish priest in just that way and who, like young John Wright, had also worked summers in the mill.

I knew of course that my own father had worked with extreme diligence all his life, though we really don't know what this means, I'm sure, until we have ourselves gone fairly well through similar experiences in our own varied sets of circumstance. My father supported a wife and five children through the Great Depression, and yet I never knew what it was not to have warm clothes in winter and I never went to bed hungry, unless punished. Our pantry was so well stocked with shelves of canned goods from S.S. Pierce (a prominent food merchant to the upper classes of the period in Boston) that I used to sneak cans of baked beans and various soups to my poor friend down at the end of the street, whose father, a lathe machine salesman, had been long out of work. My father, like Joseph, was a highly skilled man. Though unschooled at the college and engineering level, he invented the McDonnell fourdrinier, which is the most important section of any modern papermaking machine. He was a remarkable man, and the presence of the love we all had for him is still a powerful influence among those who knew him best. He told me once that he had been at the grindstone a long, long time and that he at last looked forward to a kind of retirement that would be closely integrated with those healing and restorative powers of the natural world that he had known so intimately all his life. His retirement, however, proved to be an extended denouement of quiet and patient suffering to the very end.

That word again, retirement, which frightens so many people who are on the verge of it. I prefer another word for it that is not derived from the new sociological jargon of the day, fancy terms that really mean the second half of life, and which dull experts seem to feed upon insatiably. Before getting on to my own new term for retirement, I mean to offer by way of further illustration that bit of jargonese called "parenting." My God, I can't tell you how much I despise that term. It is a term invented by clinical psychologists and no doubt highly favored by feminists, since it proceeds on the basis that fathers and mothers are suddenly interchangeable. I say they are not: a father is a father and functions as a father and a mother is a mother and functions as a mother. This is simply yet another feminist attempt to get rid of the father or hated patriarchal role.

I speak for the forgotten Josephs of this world. I also speak for the word "retreat" instead of retirement. I take the term from the sense in which the poet Robert Frost used it, especially when commending to his audiences, now and then, the Catholic practice of the spiritual retreat. He meant by this, I think, a momentary stay against confusion and a re-gathering of the forces necessary to advance once more against the darker aspects of this world. The poet was in his mid-eighties when he wrote one of his last great lyrics and which he dearly loved to read or "say" in his late public appearances. I mean the one about the lone woodsman who saw no defeat in retracing his steps through the snow in the late afternoon in order to have the strength, next day, to lay another maple low.

89

So the art of Christian aging, I think, should be something like that—a retreat for yet another blow and not just a complete withdrawal from that sweet endeavor which constitutes the very essence of life itself. If you have to grow old, of course, let it be as lustily as possible. There is probably no great harm done, after all, by those apocryphal writers and artists who have somehow left us with the impression that Joseph was an old man. Perhaps this is an extension of the image we have of Joseph in all fathers who have lived their careers to the fullness of years. Besides, only the eldering toward God can truly appreciate the idea of our later years as a strategic retreat and not just a pell-mell rout in the face of encroaching odds. It is the wisdom of retirement to conduct this strategic retreat with most of your available resources still intact. What are these available resources? They are everywhere free and there for the taking: trees that wear the changing seasons in their branches; winter birds that come to the feeder just outside the kitchen window; prayers that rise above the broken world from dynamos of contemplation; good writing and books and music and the saints in all their glory; in short, all the beauty that goes to make up the salvific grace of this world and which, at our own risk of shame, we daily corrupt and defile. In retreat, then, we have a second chance to recreate ourselves all the more fully in love and in a way we could not have fully realized while still immersed in the workaday grind of things.

An eldering Joseph is not wholly incompatible with our physical and spiritual realities in the second half of life. The ironic little secret that the hedonists of the world dare not tell you is that the diminishment of genital activity is not the greatest evil. It is in fact quite possible that Joseph, had he lived long enough, would have had the last laugh on those who have made bad jokes about him throughout the ages. The sex-hype culture seems unlikely to accept the possibility that the gradual cessation of genital activity in one's later years may well be accompanied by a sense of comparative relief. Genital activity is not all there is to any permanently loving relationship. I think that Joseph still serves us, in his always lovely and quietly dynamic way, by reminding us of an order of love which is largely disappearing from the face of the planet. If there were not something of this nature to Joseph, some sort of resolute image of fealty and human devotion, I do not think that a vigorous and strong-willed woman like Teresa of Avila would have been so attracted to him.

What we want to see maintained in Joseph primarily, I think, is the symbolic reality of the human father. In fact, I intend here to extrapolate the idea of the human father into a word in defense of God the Father, the very "Abba" of Jesus himself, now under extreme attack from the neo-Gnosticism of radical feminism and other related strains of so-called modernist thought propagated by certain priest-publicists and self-serving theologians. "Sexist language" is the new buzz term for such matters, and it is used haphazardly by certain esoteric groups and by various Sisters of the Fevered Brow who cannot tell rights from personal grievances, either real or imagined. It is an irony unperceived by these would-be "neuterists" that they have in fact made the language far more severely and unnaturally sexist than it has otherwise been in the relatively harmless use of strictly generic terms. But after a period of skitterish sensitivity to the feminist charge of rampant sexism in Holy Scripture and in the liturgy of the Catholic Church (thus far justified, if at all, in a very few minor examples), I've finally decided to chuck the charges as something woefully silly at best and simply malcontent at worst. I therefore cry, "Enough!" I have cried "Enough!" indeed when some feminist revisionists have suggested that in the Lord's Prayer we should no longer say, "Our Father," mind you, but "Our Parent," etc. Call it, then, the parenting of the Lord's Prayer, but that's the sort of nonsense we're into these days.

Let the good Saint Joseph be my guide in reasserting the legitimate role of the father not only in the life of the Church but in the life of the secular family as well. In short, I resist the wholesale attempt to foist feminist egalitarian politics on a Catholic religious tradition that has been abundantly available to such outstanding women as Teresa of Avila, Catherine of Siena, Elizabeth Seton, Mother Teresa of Calcutta, and a whole litany of most remarkable women in the Church. American Catholics are rapidly losing all sense of the Church as mystery, of the priesthood as mystery, and of sanctity itself as the most pervasive and personal form of sacred mystery. Incidentally, too, and just for the sardonic fun of it, isn't it a bit odd that Catholic radical feminists readily accept the masculine identity of Satan without so much as a ripple of dissent, whereas a male conceptualized Divinity, such as that used constantly by Jesus, is taken to be an intolerable matter? Does this begin to tell us something we dare not utter about the "neuterists" in our religious midst—that in feminism they have found at last an acceptable rationalization for their own suppressed man-hatred? Chilling, isn't it?

It is no accident that radical feminists and other neo-Gnostics are by and large, if not totally, ignorant of even the most basic anthropological studies, including, by the way, the most serious work of the late Margaret Mead. I am continually amazed by the certified deep thinkers of the age, the new theologians and revisionist biblical scholars, who are beyond grasping the facts and evidences of the demonstrable differences between the sexes. They are hard put to grasp even the obvious itself: that there are indeed but two sexes only, male and female, Adam and Eve, Mary and Joseph, which seems about as universal a fact of human existence here on earth as one can have gleaned from almost Day Six in the Paradise Garden. "Male and female he created them" (Gen. 1:27). That's all there is, folks, so forget the myth of the new androgyny.

In the name of Joseph, I reject the mischief of Catholic feminists who suddenly have a "problem with regarding God as male," according to Rosemary Radford Ruether,[1] and which may therefore result in "the ratification of traditional patriarchal theology!" (her explanation point), with the term "patriarchal," of course, always understood in the pejorative sense. Good-bye to God the Father, then, and the divine intimacy of "Abba" so loved by Jesus in His most meaningful prayers. I continue to wonder, however, why the feminists so curiously ignore the Motherhood of God and the profound mystery of Mary herself in the work of salvation, or why they are apparently indifferent to the fact that Catholic Christianity itself has, of all religions, produced the most powerful consciousness of the eternal feminine in our daily life of prayer and petition.

I once wrote a poem of petition and in celebration

---

[1] In a letter to *The National Catholic Reporter* (April 16, 1982)

of the Christmas liturgy that was published in *Spirit* magazine's anthology of poetry, *Invitation to the City* (1960), edited by the late John Gilland Brunini. I want only to quote enough of it here to indicate something of the eternal feminine in the way we invariably think about, or even contemplate, perhaps, that most tremendous event in the whole of human history which brought to us God on earth; and where Joseph comes into all this, I think, must also remind us once again of our most human and tentative origins. The poem is called "To Recreate the Scene" and has to do with the ordinary father of a contemporary household setting up the nativity scene at Christmastime:

> *Halfway in Advent*
> *We opened the cardboard box,*
> *Unwrapped the familiar figures*
> *In chrysalis of tissue,*
> *And placed them in casual fashion*
> *Upon a field of cotton snow:*
>
> *One or two sheep*
> *(Since commerce cannot contain a flock),*
> *Cattle and camels in repose,*
> *A donkey mournful as lost love,*
> *Assorted shepherds struck with wonder,*
> *The usual kings bearing unusual gifts,*
> *A few resplendent angels,*
> *And Joseph, of course—*
> *(Joseph whom we always call "of course")*
> *And Our Lady, lovely in adoration of Love.*

That's the only point I wanted to make about Joseph, Joseph whom we always call "of course" and thus take so much for granted; for, of course, he was there all the same, whether or not we have hardly noticed him. Truncating the poem at this point, arbitrarily, Joseph disappears from the scene in the same manner that he ineffably fades from the Gospel of the

94

finding of the child Jesus in the temple and is never heard of again. Though we little realize it as such, this is one of the most poignant moments in New Testament literature. In Jungian terms, it is also that moment of individuation in which Jesus realizes the developing nature of His mission on earth. Mary herself, from here on, will enter that mystery of silence which is her mission as well, and one can only intuit that Joseph's job is all but done and that no one has further need of him. More likely, perhaps, and certainly less callously, the truth is that Jesus and Mary are going to levels of interior consciousness where Joseph cannot follow.

In secular terms, this is something like that point in Shakespeare's great two-part play, *Henry IV*, where Prince Hal, on becoming king, repudiates his old pal Sir John Falstaff on coronation day. The repudiation is not only inevitable, since the boisterous days with Sir John and all the other cronies are now over and done with, but because Falstaff himself will not be able to follow where the new King Henry has to go. Therefore, freshly crowned, Henry says to Falstaff as the latter waits by the side of the road for some recognition from the king:

> *I know thee not, old man. Fall to thy prayers.*
> *How ill white hairs become a fool and jester!*
> *I have long dreamed of such a kind of man,*
> *So surfeit-swelled, so old, and so profane;*
> *But, being awaked, I do despise my dream.*

In such a manner, to this day, do we thus dismiss the old as of no longer use to us. Next to the authors of the Bible itself, I do not think that anyone has known the human heart like Shakespeare. This is not to suggest, however, that Joseph was treated with contempt.

95

He was in fact a self-effacing man and lived in the anonymity of fathers everywhere, who, having done the work they had to do, leave the challenge of the future to other hands and talents. Though it is almost certain that Joseph did not live to be an old man, we nevertheless pray to him in petitioning for a happy Christian death. I wish that it could have been so for poor, anonymous Charlie Williams who could not tolerate the idea of retirement as the ultimate isolation, the loneliness beyond endurance, and who had been left utterly uncared for by that society and industrial system which had in turn ceased to consider him a viable or negotiable commodity. I want to think that it is Saint Joseph who gathers such souls to himself and brings them into that habitation of the Lord where all sorrows cease and all true joy begins.

References and Suggested Readings

Author's Note: The theme of anonymity in the chapter on Joseph is borne out by the fact that we could find no easily available references on his life (understandably) and spirituality (less understandably).

Saint Thomas More

The Man of the World

The mark of the man of the world is absence of pretension.
— R.W. Emerson, *The Conduct of Life*

Thomas More was born in London, the son of a well-known lawyer and judge, John More, on February 6, 1478. He studied law at Oxford and was admitted to the bar in 1501, entered Parliament in 1504, and the following year married Jane Colt. Three daughters and a son were born of this union, though the beloved Jane Colt died young, and More then married the widow Alice Middleton. More soon became known as a man of great learning and a leader and reformer in the Christian humanist movement. Ironically enough, he was highly favored by King Henry VIII and served him in a succession of extremely sensitive assignments, culminating in More's appointment as Lord Chancellor of England in 1529. Thus it was at the heighth of his powers that More was suddenly confronted with the question of the King's demand to invalidate his marriage to Catherine of Aragon in order to marry Anne Boleyn, a confrontation which not only changed but ended More's life. He was beheaded on Tower Hill July 6, 1535. In literature, More is known chiefly as the author of Utopia *though he produced many other remarkable works as well. He was canonized Saint Thomas More in 1935. He is a patron of lawyers and his feast day is July 6.*

IF THE self-effacing Joseph, husband of Mary and adoptive father of Jesus, was for us the man of anonymity and perhaps the prototype of the common, hardworking tradesman and family man we recognize everywhere today, Sir Thomas More represents for us the worldly sophisticate and intellectual of great learning and influence and who may even have been a determining factor in the formation of the cultural and social attitudes of an age. I think we need this kind of person just as much as we need those who can plane good beams from the cedars of Lebanon and raise them into a lasting place. I offer the name and career of Sir Thomas More to people maturing toward God, because we cannot let go to waste the life of the mind or casually dismiss a man so principled in his Christian beliefs that he would go to the death for them. It has to be an essential part of the sacrament of Christian aging that we should hold fast to first and last principles at all costs.

With all this readily admitted and to be touched on again in due time, I want to consider Thomas More primarily as the layman par excellence, the husband and married man par excellence, and very much the father par excellence.

Unlike the anonymity in which Joseph had to live in accordance with the nature of his mission in life, Thomas More is invaluable in our own time for the assertion he represents to us of how far the Christian layman can and should go when fulfilling all his potentialities and gifts. I want people in the second half of life to be absolutely thunderstruck with the life and career of Sir Thomas More. I want you to know that he represents the best you can become in the life of the mind, in the resolution of one's principles, and in supreme fealty to conscience. He was a man who had been in the midst of it all and who still retained a marvelous wit and sense of the divine folly.

At this point, however, I am less interested in Thomas More's confrontation with King Henry VIII over the withheld approval by the Vatican and More himself, then a highly placed confidante of the court, that would have otherwise permitted Henry's divorce from Catherine of Aragon to marry Anne Boleyn, and thus also to recognize any heirs of this union as establishing a legitimate succession to the throne, etc.—I repeat I am less interested in all this than I am in the matter of More's personal integrity and the enduring relationship with his own family even under the most painful and ultimately fatal circumstances. The historical aspect of More's confrontation with the state, and all its terrible and terrifying pressures as well, may represent to us the increasing assaults that many of the elderly feel as they advance further and further into life. It is a reality that clearly contradicts the absolutely ludicrous myth that all becomes peaceful and advantageous to us as we grow older. In many instances, we become more uncertain still, buffeted by serious illnesses and always on the edge of economic insecurity and possible disaster. I am interested in how we are able to draw on such resources as will help us to resist these untoward circumstances in the way that More himself chose to stand against the onslaughts of the state.

There seems little doubt that More could not have taken his stand against the state without some very considerable spiritual resources and the purest possible convictions of intellect and conscience, but I also have the notion that the human connection with his family and friends was probably of the utmost importance to him. I have tried to determine over recent years exactly what it may be that accounts for the strength of a lasting marriage bond and which, ironically enough, seems less and less tenable in modern marriages decimated by higher and higher divorce rates. At the later stages of marriage, when genital activity has waned as possibly the most immediate and recognizable means of communication between the sexes, what is there that literally keeps a marriage together and that even may bloom like a second spring in the late autumnal and winter years? As I have said, I have thought somewhat at length and depth about this and have concluded that what is there, in the end, is something that has always been there.

I shall attempt to explain this by going back to a ten-page interview I did with Thomas Merton in 1967 for the October issue of *Motive* magazine for that year. It is an interview, though later reprinted in part by *U.S. Catholic* magazine, which has not had a wide circulation and which therefore even now remains all but unknown to most Merton enthusiasts. *Motive*, an ecumenical Methodist publication, was entirely generous in its format and presentation of the interview. At that time, of course, the famed Trappist monk (to indulge an unavoidable oxymoron) and I were not exactly strangers, having produced some five years earlier, the Harcourt, Brace & World edition of *A Thomas Merton Reader* (1962), an anthology of Merton's writings later reissued in a Doubleday Image Books revised edition (1974). Whereas that project had been formulated in several actual working conferences at the Abbey of Our Lady of Gethsemani, in Kentucky, and also involved considerable amounts of correspondence and incredible complications better left unrevealed at this time, the *Motive* interview was conducted wholly by written questions and responses. In this way, I think, Merton was all the more given to meditative and deliberate answers that probably would not have been as forthcoming in the give-and-take of normal conversation.

In any case, the point is this: I had asked Merton a question about the nature of love between a man and a woman in Christian marriage. He had himself ventured to speak on the subject in a marvelous essay titled "Day of a Stranger" in the summer of 1967 issue of *Hudson Review*, and so I thought it proper to ask him why monasticism today is still so disturbed by the seeming specter of Woman at the gate house. His lengthy reply is, it seems to me, one of the most touching revelations in the whole canon of Merton's various commentaries on life and the moral impulse in modern man. Though also a deeply poignant defense of celibacy, Merton clearly recognized in this interview what he called the radical absurdity of the celibate life itself, adding indeed that a life of man without woman is therefore an absurdity from any "normal" point of view. He spoke of the terrible loneliness of those not in direct and continuing communion with another person, loneliness as a kind of death, but which may also be present even in those who happen to share a day-to-day continuum.

Merton's remarks on human loneliness are immediate and relevant to the point at hand. There is an element of amusement, however, in the fact that Thomas More attempted to solve the problem of the loneliness of the celibate life—as against the daily rambunctiousness of domestic existence—by applying to it a typically rational approach. For several years, More lived as a guest in a Carthusian monastery (ironically, a contemplative Order that Merton himself once considered as an alternative choice to the Cistercians) while giving his days to the practice of law. It was not so much his aim to combine one way of life with the other, perhaps, as it was to make a definite choice between them by way of practical comparison. He chose marriage with Jane Colt, who bore him four children—the inestimable Margaret, Elizabeth, Cecily, and John—in just about four successive years. He was in fact so committed to marriage as a state of life that when Jane died, after an attempt to bear their fifth child, More one year later married the widow Alice Middleton as an instant replacement for the mother of his children. She was a plain woman, even blunt and rough-edged, who was described sardonically by More himself as "neither a pearl nor a girl." The household over which Dame Alice presided was nonetheless buoyant and boisterous for all that, and More went on to acquire a distinguished circle of friends and scholars in such personages as Bishop John Fisher (later a co-martyr with More), Dean John Colet, the great Desiderius Erasmus of Rotterdam, and many others, while More himself would become all the more famous with the publication in 1516 of the classic social fantasy *Utopia* and other equally forceful treatises.

I mean to suggest to people in the second half of life, especially to those who have managed to advance into the sacrament of aging in company with another person on the most intimate and confidential terms possible, that there is a clear advantage in one's having long ago become committed to a married or domestic state of life. I have myself discovered what I have come to hold as the secret advantage of the long-married over any other state of life, and I hesitate here to disclose it on the grounds that I do not want to appear insensitive to the loneliness of those who do not have available to them the means and proximity of the human encounter. I think it is one of the most tremendous of graces bestowed upon the human species that

102

we should be able simply to touch one another—the reassuring and yet ineffable human touch—the touch of hands held, or a face caressed, or of arms embracing another. I am sorry that I cannot reveal to you anything more exciting or dramatic than that: to be able to touch another human being at night or in the morning; not to have let the sun go down on one's anger or rise again in recrimination; to love the divine grace that dwells in another human soul and to have had this made manifest in something so common as a goodnight kiss, banal as that may seem to us in an age of rampant adultery and of human relationships given cheaply away, and thus to preserve as long as possible the ritual of human touch in the sacrament of aging. I cannot think of a greater loneliness in any state of life than that which does not feel the human touch after the duties and responsibilities of the day have been accomplished.

It is certain that Sir Thomas More was such a man as required the immediacy of human warmth around him and who must have daily touched the austere Dame Alice Middleton nevertheless affectionately, and it is equally certain that all his children were dear to him; especially endearing was the relationship he had with his eldest daughter, who would become well-known in her own right as Margaret Roper. We have become familiar with the relationship of Monica to Augustine, whereas it is now a nicely fortuitous counterplay to consider that of a famous father with his talented and outstanding daughter. In an age that did not consider the education of women worth the while, More saw to it that Margaret, having shown perhaps more ability than the other children, was well educated in Latin classics and philosophy. At sixteen she married the attorney William Roper, who would

103

later write the notable *A Life of Sir Thomas More*, a work perhaps more distinguished for the formality of its sixteenth-century prose than for the accuracy of its facts that were recalled from memory, years later, and from hearsay accounts at least several times removed. The letters of Sir Thomas More in general constitute one of the great collections of correspondence in the language, but the ones to Margaret in particular have about them an enduring charm and, in the last days, a terrible poignancy and starkness of ultimate truths. He wrote in Latin to his children, when they were away at school, and yearned for responses from Margaret, admonishing her not to keep the letter-carrier waiting, and even to write about nothing if there was nothing else to write about. He said that girls were chatterboxes by nature, anyway, who always have something to say about nothing at all, and would follow such banter with some of the clearest and firmest advice ever given to the neophyte as writer.

It was, however, when Sir Thomas was imprisoned in the Tower of London, for refusing to take the oath required by the Act of Succession, that the relationship between More and his beloved daughter reached its final and devastating maturity. Both Dame Alice and Margaret had taken the oath, if only to get into the Tower itself in order to dissuade Sir Thomas from holding a position that was rapidly growing untenable. It was now the twelfth of the fifteen months that would be allotted to the man of conscience in the Tower of London, and Dame Alice had just about given up trying to convince her husband to take the silly oath and live. Despite the increasing hopelessness of the situation, More himself did not attempt to impose his own convictions on any members of his family, least of all on Margaret, for she was in those last days his final and only earthly confidante. So he was all the more shocked when he one day received a letter from Margaret imploring him to submit to the wishes of the King, who would in turn instantly release perhaps the greatest Englishman of the realm, if only Sir Thomas would relent. It wasn't their having tried to save him, surely, that had at last hurt Thomas More to the very quick, but that Margaret should have attempted to violate the already painfully established integrity of his own conscience.

Nevertheless, the appeals continued and fell just as fruitlessly on ground where no one other than Sir Thomas himself could walk in that unutterable loneliness of spirit which he alone was destined to bear in all its incandescent anguish. It is ironic that in the middle of the English spring of 1535 the Tower received the added imprisonment of three Carthusian priors, as well as a learned Brigittine monk known to Sir Thomas More, and also the vicar of the scholar's abbey, all of whom were convicted on the charge that they had refused to recognize Henry VIII as "Supreme Head," the king's new title. They were condemned to be hanged and then drawn and quartered. The state considered this an extremely opportune moment to conduct what the authorities had no doubt hoped would be the final interrogation of Sir Thomas that would also lead to his release. More replied to all this that he had never wished anybody any harm, wished everyone only the greatest good, and if this were not enough to keep him alive, then "in good faith," he said, "I long not to live." On the day the three Carthusians and two other prisoners were scheduled to leave the Tower for Tyburn, the site of the executions, Margaret was granted permission to see her father again—and probably, as planned, to witness the distressful scene that was taking place just beyond the window of his cell and so convey to him the intensity of her anguish. William Roper has recorded of this moment that More used the ominous occasion as a means to humiliate himself still further before Meg, as he fondly called her, considering himself to be someone unworthily left behind while these blessed men were going to their deaths as cheerfully as bridegrooms to their marriage. It must have been in such a moment that Margaret realized fully and finally that the dreadful end was surely at hand.

At the end, indeed, it is not the great speech of Sir Thomas More at his trial that I remember, from the accounts of it by William Roper and the other biographers, nor that typically repeated line of More's to the judges of the court, and to the members of his family as well, that they should all one day meet merrily in heaven to enjoy there forever the salvific peace of the Lord—no, it is Margaret I grieve for, since in William Roper's eyewitness account of More's return from Westminster to the Tower, there is nothing that more powerfully brings to mind that passion and sacrament of the human touch which I have already described as essential to the human condition itself. Margaret is waiting in the crowd at a point which More must pass in order to enter the Tower:

". . . As soon as she saw him, after his blessing on her knees reverently received, she, hasting towards him, and, without consideration or care of herself, pressing in among the middest of the throng and company of the guard that with halberds and bills went round about him, took him about the neck and kissed him. Who, well liking her most natural and daughterly affection towards him, gave her his fatherly blessing and many godly words and comfort besides. From whom after she was departed, she, not satisfied with the former sight of him, and like one that had forgotten herself, being all ravished with the entire love of her dear father, having respect neither to herself nor to the press of people and multitude that were there about him, suddenly turned back again, ran to him as before, took him about the neck and divers times together most lovingly kissed him, and at last, with a full heavy heart, was fain to depart from him, the beholding whereof was to many of them that were present thereat so lamentable that it made them for very sorrow thereof to mourn and weep." (See *The Field Is Won*, by E.E. Reynolds, Glencoe Publishing, Encino, Calif., 1969.)

This is what I want to bring to you, as fellow travelers in the unknown territory of the second half of life, the sure reckoning and guidance of a man of principle who suffered all and gave everything he had in order to reemphasize the primacy of Our Lord and Savior Jesus Christ before all the kings of the earth. Hadn't More said himself that he was "the King's good servant, but God's first"? Again, I want you to know that in our maturing in the spirit toward God we should never give up on principles of conscience just because the end's in sight. If we see the landmarks along the horizon, all the more reason to keep a steady course and not let the wheel go spinning in our hands. People in the second half of life, it seems to me, should be holding very intense principles on the spoilation of the environment and the threat of nuclear warfare. In our Faith, indeed, our conscience should be as clearly and firmly resolved as was that of Sir Thomas More in preserving the primacy and integrity of the Church as the continuum of Jesus Christ in human history. We should not compromise ourselves, as many Catholic politicians do, on the life-killing question of abortion. We should not sit idly by as succeeding administrations of government seek more and more to undercut the only means that many of us have for living a decent, if nearly impecunious, old age.

One of my own pet irritations is the general trivialization of old age that is projected by television advertising. The subject is usually a goofy little old doll leaping suddenly into the air or trying to beat junior in one of those idiotic video computer games, etc. Television advertising seldom attempts to emulate a state of old age that could possibly bring forth the images, say, of Robert Frost, George Bernard Shaw, Leo Tolstoy, and Giuseppe Verdi (who completed *Otello* at seventy-three and *Falstaff* near eighty), the pianist Artur Rubinstein, or even famed comedian George Burns (noted for being trivialized on television as an anomaly to old age itself), and so on, though at least the latter was blessed with a piquant and saving sense of humor.

A sense of humor is indeed the last of the great virtues—and even then perhaps the greatest virtue—that Sir Thomas More so dearly exemplified to the very end of his foreshortened days. He was a truly merry man, possessing in rare abundance that finely tuned Christian virtue known as *eutrapelia*, or merry wisdom, and which, ironically enough, was in our own time so clearly evident in the life and personality of Thomas Merton (his recorded tapes of instructions to the novices at Gethsemani are the priceless materials to support this claim). But it is Thomas More himself who wins all, for he was merry still when put to the ultimate test. He had asked a sheriff's officer to help him up the steps of the scaffold, but reassured him that he could very well shift for himself on the way down. I think his spirit shot onward at that precise moment and lives with us now and forever.

References and Suggested Readings

1. *The Field Is Won*, by E.E. Reynolds. Glencoe Publishing, Encino, Calif., 1969.
2. *A Man for All Seasons*, by Robert Bolt. Random House, New York, 1962.

9

Saint John the Apostle

The Seer of Last Things

The end crowns all; and that old common arbitrator, Time,
will one day end it.

—Shakespeare: *Troilus and Cressida* (c. 1601)

John, known as the evangelist and apostle, also called "the Divine" (meaning the Theologian), is believed to have been born in Galilee in about the year 6, the son of Zebedee and Salome. A Galilean fisherman, he was the younger brother of James the Greater and with him had been mending the nets of his trade when called by Jesus to follow a new way of life. We learn something of the characters of the two brothers (Mark 3:17) when Jesus nicknamed them "sons of thunder" because of their excitable and volatile temperaments. Nevertheless, we also know from other Gospels that they were highly favored by the Lord as witnesses to the Transfiguration and on other key occasions in the life of Jesus, including that of their having been present in the Garden of Gethsemane during the agony of our Lord. It was John who ran ahead of Peter to the empty tomb on the morning of the Resurrection. It was John who recognized the risen Lord by the Sea of Tiberias and to whom the care of Mary was entrusted. He was, in later years, exiled to the island of Patmos, where, as the author of the Fourth Gospel and three epistles, he was also believed to have written the Apocalypse or Book of Revelation, the final book of the Bible. He died at Ephesus at an advanced age in about the year 100. He is represented in art as an eagle symbolizing the power and grandeur of his Gospel. His feast day is December 27.

THERE are many good reasons for selecting John the beloved Apostle as the next to last chapter in a book of saints for those maturing toward God, but the overwhelming single reason, I think, must surely have to do with his prophetic visions of the last days. We are nowhere in Holy Scripture so much compelled to consider the last days as in Saint John's Book of Revelation or, as we Catholics have it, the Apocalypse. If the nativity narrative of Luke especially may be said to be a book for one's earliest stage of life, and Matthew and Mark for our middle periods, then we who are advancing into the second half of life, either steadily or unsteadily, know in our arthritic bones that the territory is that of John's last Gospel and the Book of Revelation. We have recognized the territory.

Full confirmation of the fact would come as no surprise to us that John lived well into his nineties and was probably present at the death of the Virgin Mary, in Ephesus, where it is traditionally held that Mary herself advanced into old age (more on this in the chapter to follow). Although the miraculous manner in which John was once said to have escaped martyrdom in Rome has now been declared apocryphal, it still holds that he was the only one of the apostles who did not suffer martyrdom in fact. The point is that there is no one like John to compel us to come to terms with the prospect of our own salvation in Christ the Savior, who is the hidden yet manifest source of all human reference, and whose centrality affords the only true perspective that can give any meaning at all to our little enough lives.

Here at the beginning, however, we have to get out of the way as neatly as possible the difficulty that Roman Catholics have not been overly impressed by the Book of Revelation in the first place. It has not entered into our bloodstream, so to speak, in the way that its visceral effects are clearly evident in the preaching of the Evangelicals and the millennarian Fundamentalists. If, indeed, you have been paying any attention at all to some of those Christian Evangelical radio and television shows (God knows, they are better than all those dreadful sitcoms), you may have recognized that two of the most favored themes are (1) biblical prophecy, however outlandish, and (2) the revealed circumstances of current events, which in themselves seem to be leading to what the fundamentalists call the endtime of this world. In the first category, which derives in great part from the Old Testament, the prophetic references are almost always sourced in the Book of Daniel; in the second category, which derives from the New Testament, the chief source by far, of course, is the Book of Revelation. The reason why Daniel and Revelation are favorites of the Evangelical Christians is that each has to do with ultimate or last things and are superlatively rich in imagery and symbolism, which, in turn, leaves all the prophetic books highly susceptible to subjective interpretation.

In any event, Roman Catholics in general know very little about the matter. Heartening is the fact, however, that Catholic biblical scholarship since Pius XII's encyclical *Divino Afflante Spiritu* (1943) has exploded into such a wealth of material as to all but reestablish the Church as the major guardian of Holy Scripture in the world. Nevertheless, especially in view of this, the curious fact remains that if Catholics in general only lately seem to have acquired an increased appreciation of the Bible, their knowledge of the Apocalypse in particular is practically nil. We have heard nothing about it from either the pulpit, God knows, or the classroom. We don't even know the vocabulary. I asked a priest to explain what is meant by the Great Tribulation. He didn't know. It is all the more incredible that a priest-author of a syndicated question-and-answer column for the Catholic press, drew a complete blank in answering an inquiry on what is known to almost all biblical Christians as the Rapture and dealt instead with lower-case rapture as a reference to the mystical experiences of contemplatives and saints, etc. He simply didn't know.

Our first landlady, an old Swedenborgian turned American Baptist, would have known—and in fact, with a vengeance, did know. We were then, my wife and I, very young and very married and with nothing else to our names but three or four sticks of furniture in about as many rooms in a single-family-house on an unpaved, dusty road that came to a dead-end two or three houses down from us. The landlady, though tinged with ethereal tremors and a bit wispy around the edges of a small and angular face, was as neat as they come, determined, and full of purpose. Her particular purpose, it seemed, was to come down the front stairs just as we were returning from Sunday Mass at the small red-brick Catholic church nearby, to impart to us some of the more awesome prophecies, in the most lurid imagery possible, from what I much later realized must have been the Book of Revelation. It was a sinful world, she admonished us, through which the terrible horses of calamity would soon be galloping at breakneck speed.

As good Irish Catholics, of course, we had never heard such things; and, taken all in all, we did not find such awful and prophetic warnings very conducive to the blissful atmosphere of early marriage. She was an old and doubtlessly queer woman, we decided, so bright and early one Monday morning we started

113

looking for a new apartment. We were not ready for the Apocalypse.

When you are yourself getting along in years, however, with day after day closing in on you relentlessly, one would have to be an insensible fool not to know that something's in the wind as far as the length and breadth of our personal lives are concerned. I feel no sense of benign contempt now, God knows, for that ancient landlady who must have looked upon us as children in mortal danger. Even though Catholics are oriented more towards a sacramental than a rigidly biblical religion, it isn't a sufficient answer to lay all this at the feet of the evangelicals as their own particular preoccupation, which in a sense it may very well be, but we also have some obligations to know Holy Scripture better than we do and to increase our awareness of the varieties of authentic Christian experience that are becoming more and more visible to us by way of the electronic church. The curious fact is that much of this eschatology of the fundamentalists is perfectly acceptable. In either case, as far as Roman Catholics are concerned, the whole subject seems to have been kept a secret or is presumed to have been the exclusive territory of the specialists.

Better the territory of the specialists, however, than the casual and freely interpretive readings of the amateurs. We have in our parish a very righteous deacon—a better man by far, no doubt, than any of us—whose one-note sermon to the laity is forever tuned, droningly, to the question: "Do you read your Bible?" I've always wanted to tell him that, contrary to the generally held view that Catholics do not read Holy Scripture, we read highly selective portions of the Old and New Testaments every week and not infrequently several times a week. More than this, I'd like

114

to tell the concerned deacon that I can't imagine anything more vulnerable to both intellectual and spiritual chaos than the unguided reading of Holy Scripture; and, moreover, nowhere is this more likely to occur than in the reading of the Book of Revelation and in those particularly favored prophecies of the Old Testament that are aimed at eschatology. (Eschatology is a simply marvelous word derived from the Greek *eschatos*, meaning uttermost, and *logos*, meaning the study of or discourse thereon, and thus which has to do with such last or uttermost things as death and the general judgment, etc.). I want also to say at this point that I favor the Catholic sense of caution when it comes to the Book of Revelation, though one ought to admit just as readily that the Protestant or fundamentalist approach to it is infinitely more fun. There are radio and Christian TV shows which seem sustained almost wholly on the titillating threat, week after week, of our imminent annihilation by way of a divine edict already based on a set of familiar but esoteric prophecies, especially well-known to those who follow such scenarios.

The trouble is, of course, that the chaotic state of the world itself lends uneasy credulity to these prophecies and the possible end of the world as we know it, which is certainly a probability in the case of nuclear warfare. But there remains, all the same, a keenly distinct difference between the literal interpretations of the fundamentalists, concerning what the seer of Patmos had actually envisioned, and what this may or may not have represented in the view of a perhaps more open and even poetic wealth of ambiguity—a sense of ambiguity, indeed, all the more natural and endemic to the intuitions of Mediterranean Catholicism. A rigidly literal interpretation of Revelation is,

I'm afraid, the peculiar preoccupation of a strictly Nordic kind of Christianity.

I suppose this in itself is a merely roundabout way of saying that a Catholic attitude toward the Apocalypse—even of a lower-case catholic attitude—is more likely to witness the stupendous visions of John as the dazzling reflection of that inner reality toward which the whole meaning and substance of both the Old and New Testament writings are forever converging. I am not a theologian, God knows, but I do not think that we should trivialize John's great Book of Revelation as if it were a prepared script for an event about to take place next week—by chapter and verse—on a mountaintop clustered with tight little knots of frightened disciples waiting for the end. It is the glory of Revelation that in making all things new through Christ (John 21:5), we are joined again in something like that moment of self-creating light with which biblical literature begins. In all the annals of humankind there is no moment quite like this one, and we do not understand John at all if we do not at least intuit the Godhead itself as the perceived Alpha and Omega and as that point beyond which none may venture.

In John's writings, however, we are all points of an almost unendurable tension between the tremendous spiritual import of Revelation and the continuum of the here-and-now in which we must daily conduct the very struggle of our existence. It is only when the ego has been burned away in the long and arduous trial of living that we begin to intuit the meaning and the purity of apocalypse. Let me give you an illustration of this: I knew an excellent lady, by way of telephone conversations alone, who used to talk with me almost daily about world affairs and the state of the Church and where she thought it might be drifting in the postconciliar era. Her chief concern was what she correctly took to be the danger of secular humanism and the effect it was having among our own Priests of the Wavering Commitments, as she put it, and the Sisters of the Fevered Brow in the decades after the Second Vatican Council. However, she did not consider it a vital loss that unstable priests and nuns were jumping out of the windows which Pope John XXIII was said to have opened for the benefit of all. When she talked about secular humanism, for instance, she got down to hard cases and meant by it the specific brand of that creeping poison which is disseminated by such documents as "Humanist Manifesto II," etc., and by theories of education that are based on the new behavioral psychology. I had formed a telephonic image of her that was a combination of Dorothy Day's Christian solidity and the class, voice, and dignity of an Ethel Barrymore in her later years. A thoroughly sophisticated and intelligent woman, she'd had a notable New York City career in advertising and newspaper work and was now retired to a well-known nursing home in Boston. I came to love her dearly. She was nearly one hundred years old and longed to die, and then one day word was conveyed to me from the nursing home that her wish had at last come to pass. I remember only her wit and merry wisdom and fidelity to that lovely entity she would still have called Holy Mother the Church and would not have thought it old-fashioned to say so.

I mention my anonymous friend only because, like John the Apostle himself, who also lived nearly a century, she was granted the gifts of human intelligence to the very end—even though, in a sense, she had no further use of it beyond its capacity to cast off everything else as nonessential baggage. It was a time to travel lightly, unencumbered by the things of this world, and to leave behind only such artifacts as others may gather by the side of the road as mementos of some value. It is Saint Jerome who tells us that when John was in his last days, in Ephesus, he waxed so old and fragile that he had to be carried to the services and testimonies which he still insisted on attending and in which he was still expected to instruct the faithful. Here was John, then, the author of the Book of Revelation and other writings as well, who had at last reduced all this to the quintessential message which he repeated to the assembled people everywhere he went: "Love one another. This is the Lord's command; and if you keep it, that by itself is enough." Another version has even this much reduced to simply: "My little children, love one another," which was all he could manage to say or more than which he cared not to say.

It is in a very real sense all we need to know. We, all of us, have whole lifetimes of bitter views and deep recriminations to be gotten rid of, which, more often than not, perhaps, have been held against those we love most. When in fact you come to think of it, to love one another is just about all we have on this earth—I mean when all's said and done. John was the apostle of love, the one who is believed to have been the unidentified "disciple whom Jesus loved," and who at the Last Supper had leaned lovingly against our Lord as one in whom all the troubles of the world are soon resolved. There are few moments in New Testament literature more ineffable than that in which John, after a nighttime of luckless fishing in the Sea of Tiberias with Simon Peter and Thomas and some of the other disciples, dimly perceives at daybreak a figure on the shore. In the stillness of the early morning mist, the as-yet-unrecognized Jesus calls to them: "Children (or 'friends' in the diminutive), have you caught any fish?" They answer that they haven't, and Jesus tells them to cast their net on the other side of the boat and almost immediately they have more than a full catch.

At this point, it is John who is all but shattered in the moment of his recognition of Jesus and cries out to Peter, "It is the Lord!" Peter, true to his rude and impetuous character, also half-naked, stumbles and bumbles his way to shore in the greatest possible haste to greet his Lord and Master. On the shore, there is a charcoal fire with some fish roasting on it and some bread to go with the fish. The rest of John 21, as I have dared to say, is one of the most powerful and beautiful of all the Gospels and which has to do with the overwhelming theme of a both personal and universal love. Again, too, how curious and strange it is that in the Gospel of the resurrection morning it was John who had run ahead of Peter to reach the empty tomb; whereas, even though John had been the first one to recognize Jesus on the shore of the Sea of Tiberias, it was Peter who had thrashed through the water to greet the Lord and to see for himself whether it could possibly be true that Jesus was truly there.

It is not excessive to say that there was in all this—and, of course, still is—a weaving of the first separate strands of love that have come down to us through the centuries of history to form the Christian fabric of community and worship in the world. Redeeming love is the salvific mission of the Church, and therefore cannot be anything less than that in our own hearts. I think that we have all known people grown old who have for years and years nurtured either small or great hatreds in their hearts and minds. Bitterness in the elderly is an unseemly and smoldering fire that should have been allowed long ago to burn itself out.

119

Anger in the young is like a flare in the wind, fanned to white heat in a moment, but soon extinguished when the gusts of spent emotions cease to blow. It is never too early or too late to forgive in others the real or imagined wrongs that they have committed against us, but the greatest difficulty of all is clearly to recognize the wrongs that we ourselves have done to others. Self-knowledge is the most painful kind of knowledge, because it tends to reveal us as we really are and not as we imagine ourselves to be. What good is the accumulation of years without some increase in self-knowledge as well?

It was John the Apostle's knowledge of love acquired in the most vibrant years of his manhood, as a disciple of Jesus, that carried him serenely into the even more fully realized personhood of his own last years. In the wasteland of the moderns, we grow old in the manner of T.S. Eliot's Prufrock, wondering whether we should wear the bottoms of our trousers rolled or ought we dare to eat a peach, but for the Christian the prospect of aging is nothing less than our reentering creation through the heart and suffering of Christ. It is the chief knowledge of one's having grown older that at some ineffable point, like that in which John recognized Jesus standing on the shore of the Sea of Tiberias, we who are less than filled with such grace shall nevertheless come to realize at last that it is we ourselves who are even now peering through the morning mist to discern the luminous figure of the beloved Christ.

How soon we know that life is passing by, all the days and months and years, or maybe it is we who are passing by a standstill world. Suddenly, all that we had thought was of the utmost importance to us seems nothing more than the wind blowing through the dry

120

sea grass of a deserted beach. Instead of the charcoal fire burning on the shore, with its invitation to gather around it in fellowship and share the sparse meal of fish and bread, we shall soon have to rise and walk alone along the beach, kicking aside the beer cans and empty bottles in the sand, turning our glances from the obscene condoms floating in the oily tides, and then we shall look out toward the vast eternity of the sea's horizon and beyond, as far as one can possibly see. It was from beyond this point, indeed, that John saw Jesus transfigured, when He who shared our human nature departed this earth awhile—that little while in which we now still yearn for His miraculous and liberating return.

References and Suggested Readings

1. The Apocalypse (Book of Revelation), *The Jerusalem Bible.* Doubleday, New York, 1966.
2. *Divino Afflante Spiritu* (1943), encyclical by Pius XII.
3. John 20, 21. *The Oxford Annotated Bible* (Revised Standard Version). Oxford University Press, New York, 1965.
4. "The Love Song of J. Alfred Prufrock," by T.S. Eliot. *Collected Poems, 1909-1962*, Harcourt Brace Jovanovich, New York, 1970.
5. *Revelation*: Introduction, Translation and Commentary by J. Massyngberde Ford. The Anchor Bible, Doubleday, New York, 1975.

10
Mary

Humanity's Purest Love

Mother and maiden / Was never none but she!
Well might such a lady / God's mother be.

—Old English Carol

Mary, the Blessed Virgin, was of course born in the first century. Called Miriam in Hebrew, it is traditionally believed that she was born in Jerusalem, the daughter of Joachim and Anne in the lineage of David, though nothing certain is known either about her parentage or actual place of birth. Aside from the references to Mary in the Infancy narratives of Matthew and Luke, and only sparsely mentioned elsewhere in the New Testament, what seems fairly certain is that Mary's life was destined to remain hidden from the usual forms of worldly inquiry. The salient points of her life are the betrothal to Joseph, her impregnation by the power of the Holy Spirit, the visitation to Elizabeth, the birth of Jesus, her witness to His public ministry (in such events as the wedding feast at Cana and the finding of the child Jesus in the temple), and the consummation of His mission in the Crucifixion, where Mary is entrusted to the care of John the beloved Apostle. Her presence in the upper room at Pentecost is the last we hear of Mary in the New Testament. She probably died in about the year 48 at one of two traditional sites, Ephesus or Jerusalem, the former slightly favored because this is also thought to have been the site of John's death sometime after the Assumption of Mary into heaven, celebrated by the Church on August 15, the most prominent of the many occasions in which we pay liturgical homage to the Mother of God.

ALTHOUGH to this point we have been considering some of the saints in both their maturity and ours, with Mary now the crown and apex of all that we have said or shall henceforth dare to say, it is Jesus Christ, her Son and our Redeemer, who is the central fact of everything we have tried to suggest as a possible means to our spiritual guidance in the second half of life. It is in fact our Lord and Savior who is the most tremendous occurrence in all human existence. The world was never the same after His great and sacramental presence here had accomplished its divine mission of redeeming the human race and every individual, on a personal basis, who has accepted His salvific grace. It is the God among us who has done away with all lesser gods. If the lesser gods continue to spread their enormous confusions throughout the world, it is only because we ourselves continue to reject that original grace which has been restored to us in the redemptive action of Jesus Christ. Despite our rejection of this salvific grace, however, whether from compounded ignorance or a dangerously pernicious pride, it is a fact that the world after Jesus can never remain the same as it was before He came here, lived for awhile on a few square miles of desert, suffered crucifixion, died, was buried, and then arose in transfigured triumph to heaven—from which everlasting abode we even now await His return.

I do not say this piously and as a matter of expected form, but in the full and shattering reality of what we may now regard as the all but conclusive evidence of, yes, the Shroud of Turin as a true remnant of the most tremendous event in human history. In faith, I would continue to believe in the divinity and resurrection of our Lord without the Shroud of Turin, as indeed millions upon millions of souls have done for all

123

the centuries since Jesus rose in glory, but it would be foolish not to accept the relentlessly tested evidence of the Shroud in the apparent good faith with which it has been given to us at this particular moment in history. If you have an intuitive sense for the movement and confluence of human events, without indulging in those bizarre speculations that are frequently based on a private kind of biblical interpretation, it will not have seemed untoward to you that all human history seems rapidly to be reaching a point of irreversible importance. I do not see how it is possible to live in these times and not have some such sense of a portentous age at hand.

In saying as much, however, I only want to place in your mind the fact of Jesus as the central point around which the whole circumference of history itself revolves, or from which all being and existence emanate, even down to the least of us and upon which we must all depend. If you want to see what I mean by this sense of dependency and also the vast difference that Jesus has made both in human history and on the most personal terms possible, please look up and read a remarkable poem called "Starlight Like Intuition Pierced the Twelve," by the American Jewish poet Delmore Schwartz, which you may find in his *Selected Poems* (1967) published in a paperback edition by New Directions. In this poem, the twelve Apostles are talking about Jesus and confiding to one another that their lives will never be the same again, because of Him, concluding: "And we shall never be as once we were, / This life will never be what once it was!"

I do not think that we can come to Mary properly without realizing something of this overwhelming importance of Jesus incarnate in human history. It is no doubt easier to trivialize Mary than it is to trivialize Jesus; and if popular essays and articles about Mary are any proof of this, then I've already had my fill of them. One of the oddest references to Mary that I have ever seen may be found in an otherwise highly acceptable dictionary of saints, published in this country, which allows that Mary had played "a prominent role" in the Infancy narratives, etc. A prominent role, indeed, for we can imagine none greater on strictly human terms. I think that we diminish our own understanding and appreciation of Mary when we fail to take into consideration that she was somehow predestined in the divine plan to become the Mother of Jesus. We trivialize Mary, moreover, when we tend to think of her as just a nice Jewish girl who said yes to an angel who happened to drop in one day.The mystery of Mary is so profound, perhaps, that we are not ourselves fully given to comprehend it; and therefore treat it as lightly as possible, though in nevertheless acceptable terms. I have written a poem about this called "Little Office," in syllabic verse, which was printed in an archdiocesan newspaper:[1]

> I think of the thunderous
> silences of the Virgin
> Mary, who was given more
> than any other mortal
> to know the ultimate depths
> of man's profound reality:
>
> And yet we turn it all to
> filigree and limpid use,
> of stars and waxen roses
> we weave the image of our
> sentimental empty lives
> to clothe the Virgin's bones:

[1] *The Pilot* (Boston), September 25, 1981

I close my eyes to eclipse
the blaze of the burning sun,
and there in sunken sockets
of the visionary soul,
dark bolts of the Virgin's love
scorch my eyes to see her Lord.

Isn't it strange that, in our youth, the article of faith we are less likely to question than all others is that which has to do with the maiden who was matchless? We shall have questioned God Himself before we doubt for a moment the tenderness and loving candor of Mary. I'd not want to go on with the great bother of being a Catholic Christian, if the feminine principle in Mary the Mother of Jesus were in any way absent from, or diminished within, the wholeness and holiness that is the Church itself. Mary's is a kind of love that is still gathering force toward the end of our days. It was not ever thus, I'm afraid, since the struggle for one's faith has often been a bitter one indeed in the days of our youth, and which we hardly dare confess to ourselves in later years; and yet, after other doubts have long assailed us, the tenderness we have always felt for the Blessed Virgin Mary somehow stays with us still. Far from sentimental merely, a true love of Mary cannot be spiritually understood aside from the intuitive knowledge we must have of her as a kind of connective tissue and total affirmation subsumed in the unity and redemptive power of Jesus Christ. Mary is like the tensile strength that keeps our faith from snapping under the tugs and tensions of the world's polarities.

There is reason to believe that Mary is now coming back into her own, so to speak, but in a way that will be made clear to all of us in due time. God's declaration to Satan, ''I will put enmity between you and the woman" was the first prefiguration of Mary—as early, then, as Genesis—and the working out of that prophecy or divine edict seems to be taking place in historical time, disturbingly enough, right now. It is time to re-acknowledge the Co-Redemptrix. One may say this, of course, while still appreciating the fact that the doctrine of Mary's share in the economy of salvation has never quite left us entirely; but the richness and depth of this teaching has remained almost dormant since the Second Vatican Council in deference to the difficulties that the term Co-Redemptrix has presented to Protestants as both official observers and Vatican-watchers in general. It was largely a matter of ecumenism; but, like most ecumenism of the period, it had more to do with good manners than with any real exchange of thought and theological substance. It is ironic that the Mary of the Book of Revelation, or "the woman clothed in the sun," may bring us together in a way that even now, perhaps, we dare not foresee too clearly. There's a limit to how much clarity we can stand or how much light we may envision.

One of the profound mysteries of Mary is that we are always conscious of her essential womanliness in the same way that we do not ourselves, advancing into the personhood of our old age, ever lose the effects and influences of our own sexual identity. When we were very young, of course, we were preoccupied and perhaps obsessed with what it meant to be male and with what it meant to be female. Today we are witnessing an almost universal obsession with what it means to be a woman in the modern world—mainly, however, as this has been made manifest in a kind of medical or chemical liberation which has "freed" the nurturing sex from the biological inevitabilities of the past. Whatever else the so-called feminist movement may have gained for women in our century, the cost of it may yet prove to be too great and too destructive in too many ways. Essential to the feminist movement today are: first, the legal right to abortion (almost as the crudest and cruelest form of birth control); secondly, the use of the Pill itself (as a means of avoiding pregnancy for prolonged and even indefinite lengths of time); and thirdly, the establishing of governmental day-care centers (as a means of avoiding the personal responsibility of raising children in the first place). The feminist movement as a means of liberating women for careers heretofore traditionally closed to them, though frequently for very sound biological reasons, would still be impossible without this three-pronged set of conditions just described.

What has all this to do with Mary? Well, it is hardly a matter requiring burdensome reflection to realize a repudiation of everything that Mary represents to us. This is the most crushing kind of contradiction, especially when we pause to contemplate Mary as the principle of the eternal feminine—and, worse, that she should thus be repudiated by what the world itself calls feminism. The overwhelming characteristic that is Mary's very identity, moreover, and without which we cannot imagine her, is the profound mystery of her motherhood; and yet it is indeed motherhood itself that is being repudiated by the secularist-driven feminist movement everywhere today. Isn't it likely—more than likely, isn't it certain—that all this is something other than the merely coincidental reason for Mary's resurgence in a world that continually fails to recognize the meaning of her presence and the nature of her mission among us?

There have been extraordinary signs of Mary in the world, and yet the world at large pays no more attention to them than it does to those universal laws which send this green and blue and white-capped planet spinning through the reaches of space itself. If Mary does not remind us of the beauty of creation, in all its sacramental splendor, then we shall never have known what it was that she helped bring into creation here on earth. I am hesitant to suggest, for obvious reasons, that men are more likely than women to understand the eternal feminine and overwhelming motherhood of Mary. For example, these concepts were indeed central to some of the greatest meditations of the priest-scientist Teilhard de Chardin and should be more widely known.[2] Also, there is the Marian Movement of Priests that seems quietly and unobtrusively, but with great intensity of spirit, to be sweeping and revivifying an increasing portion of the Catholic priesthood throughout the world. I do not think that any Christian male wholly devoted to the sanctity and power of Mary could ever suggest, as a Catholic feminist has proposed, that in our enlightened century we might well call Mary "sister in the faith" instead of "Mother."[3] At least I like to think, and probably shall go on thinking, that there is in Catholic masculinity a supremely Christian intuition for the motherhood in Christ of the Blessed Virgin Mary.

It will be at an inconceivable cost that we suffer the loss in this world of the universal role of motherhood. That marvelously feminine disciple of Carl Gustav Jung and a convert to Catholicism, Jolande Jacobi, asks in her excellent treatise *Masks of the Soul* (1976): "Is it not alarming when fewer and fewer mothers understand the souls of their children and

---

[2]*The Eternal Feminine*, by Henri de Lubac. Harper and Row, New York, 1971.
[3]Patricia Noone in *Mary for Today*, Thomas More Press, Chicago, 1977.

hide their helplessness behind excessive severity only to see them turn out as weaklings or neurotics? Or when youth, deprived of guidelines, and more iconoclastic than ever before, falls victim to slogans for want of living examples? Young people who never grow up, adults who do not know how to age, old people who painfully cling to youth—this is the unvarnished portrait of our era."[4] Dr. Jacobi has the sense and reality of this exactly right, I think, and all the more devastating in her succinct and cogent observations on our almost tragic inability, at any stage of life, to deal with what has become for us the problem of one's spiritual and moral growth.

Growth has become a problem for us only because we have already assumed that growing old is the greatest evil. What we mean by this, I suppose, is that at some point or other we suddenly become conscious of the burden we must carry around with us in all these little bundles of constricting tissues attached to the creaking bones of our arrested mobility. Despite such suddenly acquired restraints, however, there is nothing to stop the spirit from shooting on toward realms of development where the body cannot follow. It is this shifting of the gears that inevitably leaves behind those who cannot grow in the spirit and who merely become all the more embittered at that point where the body itself had begun to break down. At this point, indeed, I want again to call on Father George W. Rutler and his remarkable little book, *The Impatience of Job*, which we cited in our earlier chapter on Job himself as the recipient of all possible human ills—and, consequently, as a guide to the process of ag-

[4]*Masks of the Soul*, by Jolande Jacobi. Translated by Ean Begg. Wm. B. Eerdmans. Grand Rapids, Mich., 1976.

ing under duress. Consider in amazement, then, the following passage:

> It is hard to think of Jesus as an old man, bruised with the years, stretching and dying in senility on the cross. Jesus must have had to be young to make clear that his death was inflicted by human arrogance, his last breath not the gasp of old age but the gasp of a fighter and his death not a segment of evolution but a signal of revolution. But that is also why Mary, in the same sense, had to die of old age. She is the model of the human race in its perfect response to God's activity in history and time does take its toll on her; she is the purest expression of how to grow old.

What a marvelous meditation that is, for what else is meditation itself but an adventure of the spirit in exploring the new territories which we have dared to enter. It is true, which is to say it conforms to the divine economy of things, that Jesus could not have died as an old man racked upon the cross. What is less likely to have occurred to us, however, is Father Rutler's observation that Mary must have lived out her life in full, though we seldom think of her as anything other than a young and most lovely woman who was one day swiftly assumed into heaven in order to escape the ravages of old age.

Maybe it is just as reasonable to presume that Mary could have lived a long and hidden—which is to say, contemplative—life in the divinely assigned care of John the Apostle in Ephesus. Of course, too, we must dare to meditate on this still further: that is, suddenly to realize that our Lord's admonition from the cross was indeed reciprocal: Not only, "Woman, behold thy son," but also, "Son, behold thy mother." The suffering of Mary at the foot of the cross was of so unfathomable a nature that none of the disciples—not

131

even the beloved John—could have either perceived or suffered it in quite the same way; and therefore it was Mary herself who then became the mother of the disciples (hence her presence in the upper room) and probably of John in particular.

What we do know, however imperfectly, is that something more was taking place at the foot of the cross than a simple exchange of filial and maternal responsibilities that would have ordinarily ensued after the death of Jesus. As Prof. John McHugh suggests in his excellent study, *The Mother of Jesus in the New Testament* (1975), it is in John that we must come to recognize the prototype of those in the world who love Jesus. In an even more profound sense, it is Mary who therefore becomes the mother of all who love Jesus; and it is particularly significant, in this regard, that in Mary's eyes we have ourselves become as the little children she cannot suffer to see separated from her Son. The element of childlikeness is essential, I think, in our whole relationship to Mary. We cannot go on thinking that nothing much happened to Mary after the Annunciation and birth of Jesus, when in fact the suffering of Mary at the foot of the cross was of such hidden and profound consequences that it would set the pattern of Christian community for all earthly time. We can now see that Father Rutler is clearly on the right track, for it was no doubt absolutely necessary that Mary should have lived a long life in the spiritual surveillance and protection of her children as they continued to form the early Church, one divinely inspired way or another, and which later generations would fondly and truly call Holy Mother the Church.

It would be a most grievous error—almost, as it were, a fatal misunderstanding of Christianity itself—to think of Mary as a merely passive woman, taciturn and demurely withdrawn, whereas she is in fact the most vibrant of all human beings ever to have lived at all, the most affirming and subtly forthright, the one altogether most set against the evil powers of this world, and in whom the sufferings at the foot of the cross are still extended into the vilest rejections, by the modern world, of her Son Jesus Christ. We need Mary more than ever, surely, as we advance toward that time when we shall have fully recognized her as the woman clothed in the sun, the woman envisioned by John on Patmos, and perhaps we shall know as well why she and John have been so closely linked together in that dominion of life which is the lordship of Christ Himself. I cannot understand why types of harassing Catholic feminists today are trying to force a Gnostic concept upon the Divinity when the principle of the eternal feminine, as Teilhard de Chardin called it, is so profoundly present in the Blessed Virgin Mary. One of the most beautiful of paradoxes in the New Testament, I think, is that in which we no longer hear of Mary after the literally stunning event of Pentecost in the upper room; and yet it is she to whom is consigned the protection and pristine integrity of priesthood derived from the apostolic succession itself down to our own day.

In closing these remarks on the sacrament of Christian aging, we have only to remember that in Mary is the perfect culmination and also the reconciliation of all those variously human aspects that are present in the great and beautiful saints we have chosen to represent, in all possible humility, throughout this book. The highest state that we can attain in our metamorphosis of Christian aging is to have become like spiritually revivified and intellectually mature little children again—no, not again, for we do not want to be the children we were, but children of a manifestly new kind. So it is essential that as we grow older, we should become younger and younger in the Holy Spirit that continues to breathe through us the very élan of our perilous existence—more than our existence even, our very being. The goal of our becoming, then, is the sense and actuality of being in which, as Saint Augustine said, we shall have found no rest until we rest in thee, O God, source of all beauty so ancient and new.

I thank the saints who have helped us along the way: Monica, who loved persistently; John Vianney, who listened well; Teresa, who loved intensely; Jerome, who loved madly; Francis, who praised creation; Job, who suffered; Joseph, who provided; Thomas, who sacrificed all for principle; John the Apostle, who proclaimed the Word; and literally above all, Mary, mother of all Christians, the woman clothed in the sun, whose beams of radiant light illuminate nothing if we do not see in them a pure reflection of that one ineluctable Light who is forever our Lord and Savior Jesus Christ in all His risen glory.

References and Suggested Readings

1. *Selected Poems*, by Delmore Schwartz. New Directions, New York, 1967
2. The Pilot (Boston), Sept. 25, 1981.
3. *The Impatience of Job*, by George W. Rutler. Sugden, Sherwood & Company, La Salle, Ill., 1980.
4. *The Mother of Jesus in the New Testament*, by John McHugh. Doubleday, New York, 1975.

11
Living in the Second Half of Life

An Afterword

I HAVE always been fascinated by the attitudes of gifted men and women advancing into old age, whether sacred or profane, and we are all gifted in one way or another. Some more than others, no doubt, but gifted nonetheless in our own peculiar ways. The problem of growing old is that as role models par excellence—that is, by virtue of the fact of survival itself—we have also to deal with the preservation of our human dignity in the face of diminishing powers, to say nothing of diminishing odds. How to "go gentle into that good night," the poet Dylan Thomas to the contrary, is the heart and soul of the matter; and by going gently I do not mean either passively or lethargically, but with something of that sense of order and serenity which the lonely traveler may experience in having reached the hospitality of a good inn just before dark.

Speaking of serenity, the brilliant British essayist and literary critic V.S. Pritchett, one of the vanishing men of letters still writing today, has said about that elusive quality which none would have dared to mention when we were young: "Whatever there is to be said for serenity, there is not much opportunity for it in the modern world; and indeed I know by watching myself that old people are liable to fantasies of sadistic vengeance." And added almost by way of afterthought: "The old should not look at the news on television at night." I have taken these remarks from some half dozen tear sheets I had filed away that featured Pritchett's essay, "Looking Back at 80."[1] Pritchett on old age is far more sardonic than anything you can find in the luminous serenities of Malcolm Muggeridge and even warns his readers, suspecting in them perhaps a Sunday supplement kind of optimism, "I have no religious faith."

Religious faith, however, is the very essence of that common predicament for which old age itself is the ultimate preparation. If Pritchett takes religious faith to mean the dull pieties of mere religiosity and those arbitrary routines into which parts of our sacred liturgies have fallen, then he does well to avoid these effects. But if he means to denigrate the universal impulse in our human experience to know something more than we can wholly perceive within the limitations of our material imprisonment, then I think him sadly mistaken and the prisoner of his own prejudices. It is ironic that what Pritchett recognizes as the condition of serenity—and what else if not serenity of soul?—may also be seen in what the moral theologians call a state of grace.

This precisely, in fact, is what the great Swiss psychologist C.G. Jung has perceived as "perfect serenity of soul, a creative equilibrium, the source of spiritual energy."[2] Jung has clearly recognized the importance of a religious view in preparation for the end of one's days in what he calls the second half of life.

[1] *The New York Times Magazine* (December 14, 1980).
[2] *C.J. Jung Speaking: Interviews and Encounters,* edited by William McGuire and R.F.C. Hull, Princeton University Press, Princeton, N.J., 1977.

The psychology of the second half of life is one of the great contributions of Dr. Jung to interior knowledge and to the quintessential care of human beings. Jolande Jacobi (d. 1973), who was one of the foremost interpreters of Jungian psychology and a convert to Catholicism, said: "One of the main reasons I came to Jung's psychology is the great concern it shows with the problems of the second half of life."[3] It was Jung, she adds, who advocated schools for adults into the thirty-fifth to fortieth years—in short, literally speaking, for that second half of life which becomes so different from the first and in which we begin to shed the personas or masks we wear when attempting to realize ourselves into something we have not yet achieved—and, in all probability, never shall achieve, for such is the nature of our life that it should remain so strewn with the debris of broken dreams.

The second half of life, Dr. Jacobi says, permits us to stand up for what we really are and will have become: "One sometimes sees on the faces of mature old people their individual, untypical expressions, which show that they are now able to be natural and let themselves go. During the course of life, the ego has become more secure. One has come to terms with his own strengths and weaknesses and no longer wishes to play a part at all costs or gain power." Dr. Jung and Dr. Jacobi have both emphasized the tragedy of young people who never grow up and of "adults who do not know how to age," but who pathetically cling to youth, as if youth itself were the immediate source of that order of wisdom which we can acquire only from having lived in the first place. I can personally testify to Dr. Jacobi's marvelous insights regarding our coming to

[3]*Masks of the Soul,* Wm. B. Eerdmans, Grand Rapids, Mich., 1976.

terms with ourselves in the second half of life and of wishing no longer to strive for power at all costs. I have seen all the grim young men on the commuter trains going into the city (and not so long ago was one of them myself), each armed with his briefcase and quarter-folded morning newspaper, and I have winced for these very earnest young men and women thus engaged in the acrimonious and futile wars they must wage every day and then go home to places distraught with the added problems of modern domestic life all around them.

The growing old, however, have their problems too. The person in the second half of life must avoid acquring illusions of another kind. I would engrave the following two sentences by Dr. Jacobi on the Social Security cards of all Christians going into retirement: "A good Christian has been taught that life, far from being that which leads us into the bright fields of eternal bliss here on earth, presents us rather with the strength and opportunity to learn to bear the pain and tensions it constantly afflicts us with through the knowledge that our burdens are the inevitable consequences of expulsion from paradise. This knowledge is today largely forgotten, though it is the only way to inner peace." Read "expulsion from paradise," if you are not a strict literalist of Holy Scripture, as the loss of innocence in youth or even in the belief that youth itself is forever paradise. In any case, what Dr. Jacobi is pleading for here—as did her mentor Carl Gustav Jung—is at least some initial awareness that maturity in old age is impossible without our having experienced, at least to some degree, the chastening effects of self-knowledge.

In an interview with an English journalist, anticipating the eighty-fifth birthday of the great psychiatrist in 1960, Dr. Jung said: "An ever-deepening self-knowledge is, I'm afraid, indispensable for the continuation of real life in old age, no matter how unpopular self-knowledge may be. Nothing is more ridiculous or inept than elderly people pretending to be young—they even lose their dignity, the one prerogative of age. Looking outwards has to be turned into looking into oneself. Discovering yourself provides you with all you are, were meant to be, and all you are living from and for" (*C.G. Jung Speaking*). He meant life to be lived as an "unrepeatable experience," which may be another way of saying, I suppose, that there can be no self-discovery in stasis.

In any case, let no one be scared off by such clinical—and, worse, inspirational—terms as self-knowledge and self-discovery, etc. The point is that only with some amount of pain can we shed the cherished and protective illusions we have had about ourselves. To stand naked to one's enemies is not half so bad as standing naked to oneself, though it needn't be all that embarrassing for more than a moment or two of rare enlightenment. Many years ago I fell in love with a small book titled *The Measure of My Days*, by Florida Scott-Maxwell, a perfectly marvelous woman, who, at eighty-three, bequeathed a lovely wisdom to this perverse and skeptical world. The literary critic and American man of letters, Malcolm Cowley, cites her work as well in his own *The View From 80*, quoting this: "I want to tell people approaching and perhaps fearing age that it is a time of discovery. If they say—'Of what?' I can only answer, 'We must find out for ourselves, otherwise it won't be discovery.' "

Exactly. And so what I say here ought to be taken as a kind of finding out for oneself. Something you find out immediately is that you stay an individual, all the same, and what I find that suits me may not suit you. For myself, then, I have discovered four qualities or conditions that seem to me essential for exploring the terrain of the unknown territory ahead: (1) Interest, certainly, or Curiosity; (2) Enthusiasm; (3) Eutrapelia; and (4) Meditation. There is a natural progression or relationship in these conditions, especially in pairing them off, and which may thus reveal to us the fact that a continuing interest, for example, is well-nigh impossible without some degree of enthusiasm to sustain it; and that a sense of well-being ought to be required for even the most rudimentary stage of meditation. Though applied in different ways by different individuals, I do not see how anyone can enter the youth of old age—or, for that matter, the old age of youth—without all these conditions well-stocked in one's psychic knapsack. Let us apply these categories to the lives and careers of four individual representatives.

—J.R.R. Tolkien, the great British linguist and creator of *The Lord of the Rings* trilogy and other works, personifies for me that quality of interest or curiosity that is necessary for the growth of mind and spirit at any point in life. Generally speaking, our spiritual development is badly flawed when we continue to be unduly influenced by the things of our youth and thus fail to take on the even greater influences of our maturity. Let your interests begin to extend well beyond your family circle and private rooms. At your age, yes, take out a library card and go to the library often, preferably in the morning when all the schoolkids are safely ensconced in their classrooms, and you will find it an enchanting place to be. Go to the district courthouse and listen to some of the arraignments and hearings there and you will find, perhaps, that even at this late date you have been leading a rather sheltered life. There's nothing like a lively sense of interest to prevent stagnation from setting in. Thoreau, who was for me clearly the preeminent author of my youth, seems somehow diminished now with the advance of years, and of many changes of rebellious views merely, and so I read the venerable W.H. Hudson instead. I now read John Ruskin instead of Emerson, *The Tempest* instead of *Romeo and Juliet*, and so on. And yet it was the steadily maturing Tolkien who, well into the second half of life, created a world of fantasy and linguistic invention for whole new generations of the young who would be reading him long after his death, in 1973, at eighty-one.

—Hokusai (first name, Katsushika), the great Japanese artist and color printmaker whose life spanned the last part of the eighteenth century and nearly the first half of the nineteenth, is my own candidate for the total personification of enthusiasm. Enthusiasm, of course, is simply a manifestation of interest that cannot contain itself. It helps to have a touch of genius in order to balance the enthusiasm, which might otherwise appear to be merely giddy in the middle-aged and downright foolish in the old, but a well-tempered enthusiasm is not an untoward quality to have in the second half of life. I discovered an Irish poem that prompted me to muse: "Ah, when you write a poem like that, my friend, you may sweep the streets of Dublin for the rest of your life and still be a king." That's living with enthusiasm, however quietly, as did Hokusai less quietly, perhaps, until he was nearly ninety years old. He was himself an insatiable creator and claimed that he had not really learned to paint until he was nearly old enough to die, and so he then painted all the more madly in his last years and was in fact known

141

as "The Old Man Mad for Painting." You have no doubt seen reproductions of one of his greatest drawings, without even knowing it, that singular "Great Wave" at the apex of its crest and the white foam of it just beginning to break off on the downward curl. It is the perfect wave that surfers seek. All in all, Hokusai was a total enthusiast of the creativity of the human spirit.

—Thomas Merton has always epitomized for me the quality of *eutrapelia,* a more or less rare theological term (from the Greek) that means nothing more frightening than a kind of "merry wisdom" or "grave merriness," which is usually associated with someone more advanced in age than that attained by the Cistercian gadabout at only fifty-three. He was, however, at the time of his death, well into what Jung had called the second half of life. It has been scarcely remarked of Merton, even in most of the books produced by the new Merton research industry, that his sense of merry wisdom was an essential part of his character and personality. It is almost amusing that so many critics are taking him so grimly today. I have said elsewhere as well that the best available source for witnessing this merry wisdom of Thomas Merton, oddly enough, may be found not so much in the many literary works, as such, but all the more, I think, in what we may now hear on the tapes he recorded during his lectures to the novices and others under his spiritual guidance at the Abbey of Gethsemani. Other "eutrapelians" of Christian maturity are Malcolm Muggeridge, of course, and the lesser known Rahner—Hugo, priest and brother of Karl—and author of the highly relevant *Man at Play* (1967). Another essential Christian eutrapelian is Joseph Pieper in his classic little study on a theory of festivity, *In Tune With the World* (1965). You will know what eutrapelia means when you realize that Hans Küng, for example, doesn't have it.

—Teilhard de Chardin is not likely to be everyone's choice to exemplify a quality of authentic meditation in the second half of life, but he is clearly mine; and this mainly by virtue of *The Heart of Matter* (1976), in its English translation, his crowning achievement, which he wrote when he was sixty-nine and only five years away from his own death, in 1955, on Easter Sunday in New York City. I choose Teilhard because he ranges the whole of creation, from microcosm to macrocosm, and opens up to me a Creator who fills our vision of the universe with wonder and incredible awe and with more than a touch of holy fear. I would prefer to remain sheltered in the quiet and luminous prose of a John Henry Newman, whose meditative sonorities have held me in thrall all my adult life, but I nevertheless must go on with what I take to be the advance of Catholic Christian thought in the best and truest writings of Teilhard de Chardin. Besides, the greatest meditative writings of our century, despite those of Merton and a few others, do not happen to be in English. In addition to *The Heart of Matter*, there are the contemplative writings of Raissa Maritain, Adrienne von Speyr, and Hans Urs von Balthasar's little known *Heart of the World* (1954), with its similar title to Teilhard's masterpiece, and possibly the single finest spiritual work of our time.

In the end, however, let us face the fact that our mortal enemy is loneliness—and, worse, boredom. The classic American statement in fiction of the loneliness and despair of old age is Willa Cather's *My Mortal Enemy* (1926). I think I knew that poor dying woman, Myra Henshawe, as she cried out in the muted anguish of her own dark night of the soul, "Why must I

143

die like this, alone with my mortal enemy!'' (notice the exclamation point instead of the question mark)—and that enemy, of course, not only death but herself as well—and drawn in that image I shall always have of her, through the power of Willa Cather's prose, of an old woman wrapped in blankets and sitting alone against the trunk of a cedar tree on a cliff by the sea. So I think we must Christianize that potentially destructive moment which Pritchett calls the "great distress of old age" in the death of friends and "the thinning ranks of one's generation"—I say we must Christianize this into something better, even if it means a weaning away from the exclusive concerns of this world as we were once weaned toward it in a good and nurturing way. The journey, again, must remain directed toward self-knowledge so that our own once very strong and perhaps wholly self-centered free will may be subsumed at last in the Will of God. Those momentary stays against confusion mentioned above—interest, enthusiasm, eutrapelia, and meditation—are simply some of the essential conditions that will make the journey into the second half of life a little easier; and I have peopled or personified these abstractions against the loss of friends as we ourselves grow older.

Here is a passage I want you to know from one of the truly outstanding books of our time, C.G. Jung's *Memories, Dreams, Reflections* (Pantheon Books, New York, 1963), as recorded and edited by Aniela Jaffe and translated by Clara and Richard Winston. Dr. Jung was eighty-one when he allowed the telling of his own life story to be put down on paper and eventually arranged into a book that has turned out to be one of the great modern autobiographies. It's proper too that we should approach the end of these essays

144

with Jung in mind, somewhat as we began with him, in his healing concept of the second half of life. Here, then, is the last paragraph of the essay, "Retrospect," in whose penultimate paragraph Jung had also recognized both the cruelty of the world into which we are born and its divine and redeeming beauty as well. It is at this point that Jung reveals:

"When Lao-tzu says, 'All are clear, I alone am clouded,' he is expressing what I now feel in advanced old age. Lao-tzu is the example of a man with superior insight who has seen and experienced worth and worthlessness, and who at the end of his life desires to return into his own being, into the eternal unknowable meaning. The archetype of the old man who has seen enough is eternally true. At every level of intelligence this type appears, and its lineaments are always the same, whether it be an old peasant or a great philosopher like Lao-tzu. This is old age, and a limitation. Yet there is so much that fills me: plants, animals, clouds, day and night, and the eternal in man. The more uncertain I have felt about myself, the more there has grown up in me a feeling of kinship with all things. In fact, it seems to me as if that alienation which so long separated me from the world has become transferred into my own inner world, and has revealed to me an unexpected unfamiliarity with myself." At which point, clearly, Jung had already reached the wisdom of that self-knowing toward which we all strive.

It is, at length, in the second half of life when we come more and more to realize that our place here on earth is no lasting home, no matter how well we may have built or how long we have ourselves endured, for we live as in tents pitched against the wind. What treasures we have laid up on earth are as nothing to those that are offered to us freely by the recreating earth

145

itself, though in piecemeal fashion, at the end of days. I remember lately one such day in the first warm rains of March, when my wife and I stood in the kitchen doorway and watched the mourning doves in the pine and oak trees at the back of the house, at least a dozen of these soft and beautifully sculpted birds, taking what finally dawned on us were baths and showers in the quietly falling rain. I saw this alone, at first, watching from my bedroom window in the morning. A dove would lift its wing and extend it as far as possible in the vertical position, hold it there a moment, let it down slowly and then raise the other wing in exactly the same manner. I was so struck by the pale and almost luminous mother-of-pearl beauty of the under-wings that it did not occur to me what in fact was really going on there. Then, on another branch, another dove would raise its wing and thus perform the same ritual of the extension and lowering of the wing, then another and another, until whole branches of the trees in the soft spring rain seemed to shimmer and come alive with the ritual of cleansing and purgation after the long, inhibiting winter.

The lesson for today, friends and neighbors, is that our existence in the second half of life must finally be seen as something like the return to, and reimmersion in, that vast and at the same time very particularlized sacramentality of God's holy creation from which we had emerged in the first place, only minimal years ago, though now impelled forward with a conscious-ness of soul that trembles in the delight and antici-pation of union with the Trinitarian reality. In the sec-ond half of life, therefore, we do not live any the less, I think, but all the more. "There is more day to dawn," said my neighbor Henry Thoreau of Concord, more than a century ago, and thought himself a worthy and independent man unencumbered by any hint of the Christian virtues; and yet in whose countless pages of writings there are abundant biblical references that reflect his cultural origins like bits of mica in rocks turned toward the sun. But in the end he could not hold a candle to that full blaze of sacramental light which shines forever in the works of Dante, Saint Francis, and the poet Gerard Manley Hopkins. For it is in the second half of life that we do not seek alienation but a kind of kinship with universal entities—that kinship, in short, which must be resolved finally and wholly in the redemptive power and salvific kingship of Our Lord Jesus Christ. Amen.

References and Suggested Readings

1. *The Measure of My Days*, by Florida Scott-Maxwell. Knopf, New York, 1968.
2. *The View From 80*, by Malcolm Cowley. Penguin Books, New York, 1982.
3. *Tolkien: A Biography*, by Humphrey Carpenter. Houghton Mifflin, Boston, 1977.
4. *A Thomas Merton Reader*. Revised edition, Edited by Thomas P. McDonnell. Image Books, Doubleday, New York, 1974.
5. *The Heart of Matter*, by Teilhard de Chardin. Translated by Rene Hague. Harcourt Brace Jovanovich, New York and London, 1978.
6. *Man at Play*, by Hugo Rahner, S.J. Preface by Walter J. Ong, S.J. Seabury, New York, 1967.
7. *In Tune With the World*: A Theory of Festivity, by Josef Pieper. Translated from the German by Richard and Clara Winston. Franciscan Herald Press, Chicago, 1973.
8. *My Mortal Enemy*, by Willa Cather. Knopf, New York, 1967.
9. *Memories, Dreams, Reflections*, by C. G. Jung. Edited by Aniela Jaffe. Translated by Clara and Richard Winston. Pantheon Books, New York, 1963.